Small Footsteps In The Land Of The Dragon

Growing Up In China

Barbara Brooks Wallace

Copyright © 2016 Barbara Brooks Wallace

All rights reserved, including the rights of reproduction in whole or in part in any form.
An imprint of Pangea Publishing
ISBN-10: 0-9894065-4-7
ISBN-13: 978-0-9894065-4-3

DEDICATION

To Victoria, (aka Boo), Ross (aka Ross) , Elizabeth (aka Bizzy),
and my very special Pen Pal,
Blythe Bunnee (aka Blythe Abigail Su-Ren Schulte)

PREFACE

Growing up in China! People often ask if I liked growing up in China. Did it feel different? Different from what? How could it feel different if the sights and sounds, and, yes, even the pungent smells had always been there in my life from the time I was born? Now, looking back on it, I suppose I can see where it was different compared to growing up in America, and perhaps can understand why people might ask. But it wasn't different back then. No, it wasn't then at all.

Even when we were caught up in the swirl of things happening in China on a national scale, the Communist uprising, the attacks by Japan that presaged World War II, things that actually affected my life more directly in one way or another, I was only a child busy with growing up in my own little world, taking my own personal small footsteps in the Land of the Dragon.

SMALL FOOTSTEPS IN THE LAND OF THE DRAGON

Soochow The Beginning, And Boy, Coolie, Amah, And Pidgin.... 1

Tsinan Love Affairs, No Kindergarten, And Warlords 7

Hankow The Ching Ming, Summers, And A Leather Slipper 13

Hankow Continued British School Rules, Riots And Witch Hunts 21

Hankow Home Leave A King, A Patsy Ann Doll, And An Indian Giving Lesson 27

Tientsin, No. 1 Newchwang Loo Stairs, Weddings, A Funeral, And A Vampire Remedy 31

Tientsin Spit, Smells, China Sounds And School 45

Sisters, Funnies, The Boys, Wonks, And Saturdays 61

Peitaho Dusty Streets And Donkeys Seashells, Sunsets And A Glassy Sea 75

Peitaho Still Of Mice And Sadness And A Scary Journey 89

Shanghai Sas, And Peitaho Redux 97

Peitaho Farewell Of "Incidents", Us Two, And The U.S. Navy 105

Between China And Philippines Cruising On The USS Chaumont 115

The Philippines Baguio, Boarding School And Baloots 123

China The Closing Curtain 129

A LOOK BACKWARD 133

CHAPTER I

Soochow
The Beginning, And Boy, Coolie, Amah, And Pidgin

It is 9:00 o'clock one Sunday morning in the Year of the Dog, in Soochow, China. My father is struggling to climb into his trousers, and all the while moaning to himself, "Omigosh! Nicia's dying!"

That is, at least, what I've always been told. Of course, Nicia, my mother was not dying at all. She was simply upstairs in their bedroom having me. My father must have heard a little moan, or squeak, or some kind of proper noise that it seems to me my mother was allowed to make under the circumstances.

Father had at least had the presence of mind to send Boy with a chit for the missionary doctor who was to have been present at the event, but instead was attending church services.

"How could he have gone off to church that morning and not stayed at home waiting for me to arrive?" I asked Mother years later when I was told this story. I don't believe I ever had a satisfactory answer to this question, probably because there wasn't one.

"By the time the doctor finally did arrive," Mother said, "I had sent Coolie off to fetch boiled water, delivered you myself, and had you cleaned and wrapped in flannel like a little cocoon."

The doctor examined the two of us and said we were both in fine shape. Then he returned downstairs and administered to Daddy, who was in a state of collapse, and the only one needing his attention.

Well then, maskee, never mind, I thought, it wasn't a wasted trip after all, and justified his leaving the Sunday church service. It was all so quick; I wouldn't be surprised to know that the congregation hadn't even arrived at the final hymn.

This event took place in a house I only knew from two small snapshots. In them I see a drab looking box of a brick, two-story house sitting alone by the Soochow Creek. It is surrounded by a grim wall topped with shards of glass like a spiked guardian dragon. But this must not have offered much comfort to my mother. While my father was off on a donkey cart, accompanied only by his Chinese translator, to sell oil for the lamps of China for the Standard Oil Company of New York (SOCONY), my mother slept with a gun under her pillow.

She had been advised to go to Shanghai to await my arrival, but she did not want to leave my sister, Connie, then only fourteen months old, even in the care of her devoted baby Amah.

People have often said to me, "I suppose your mother could do what she did because she was a nurse." Yes, I suppose so. But then knowing what to do when what is happening is happening to someone else, is quite different than when it is happening to you. One might as well suppose a surgeon could remove his own appendix because he's a surgeon, taking into account, of course, the obvious differences in the procedure. I know also that Chinese peasant women in those days were known to go out into a field alone to have their babies.

But I still think my mother was able to deliver me so successfully because of the kind of person she was. Being a nurse was only part of it. Anyone who knows her story of leaving Russia as a sixteen-year-old, going to Shanghai, and finally graduating as a nurse from the Harvard Medical of China, would have to agree.

As for me, uncomplicated as my birth was, I turned out to be a scrawny little thing, and quite a contrast to my cheerful, curly-haired, chubby sister, Connie, who had gurgled and cooed through her babyhood, while I screamed my head off with colic. The state of my health was to be a worry to my parents for years. Furthermore, I certainly could not have given any promise of adding to the reputation Soochow had, besides being considered the Garden City of China, of producing the most beautiful women in China, assuming they were all beautiful babies at birth.

"You were both named after movie stars," Mother always told my sister and me. That was all well and good, but I never felt being named after glamorous movie stars accomplished much, not where I was concerned at any rate.

But I will leave me in that unhappy noisy state for a moment for a necessary explanation because I see that though my story has barely started, I have already mentioned Boy, Coolie, and Amah. They were our servants, and so much a part of our lives as children that it is impossible to think of growing up in China without them. They were for us a kind of extended family.

"You must have been terribly rich to have all those servants," relatives and friends in America said.

"No, we weren't rich at all," we always replied. "In China everyone has servants." But nobody really believed us. It did no good to explain that in China of those days having servants was a way life.

Boy, called simply that or sometime by his first name, was the equivalent of a head butler. Families who were indeed rich, or at least much richer than we were, more often than not had several Boys, Number One Boy, Number Two Boy, and so on. Naturally, Number One Boy was a very powerful person in a household. His position gave him a great deal of "face." Our family never had more than one Boy, of course, so we didn't have to worry about numbers.

Coolie was the man who performed the more menial duties in the house. Cook almost always went by the name of Dossofoo, or "man of important business." And then there was Amah, a Chinese "nanny" always faithful, devoted, loving children, never letting a child in her charge out of her sight for a moment, and ready to protect that child with her life. It was a rare child of China who did not love his or her Amah.

About the word "maskee." It was a long time before I stopped using that word and others like it, and puzzling American friends with it. It wasn't intentional. It just ran in my blood, and it took me a long time to lose it. The word is Pidgin . . . Pidgin English.

"Why did you and Daddy never have us learn Chinese?" I asked my mother in later years. "Why were all our servants required to speak English?"

"That was because Daddy and I didn't want you to pick up all those 'naughty' Chinese swear words," said Mother.

The result of that bit of silliness was that we grew up not able to speak the Chinese language except for a few good Chinese words such as sheh-sheh, for "thank you," but along with all the other "little darlings" in China possessed a whole verbal dossier of pungent Chinese expressions. They were picked up, where else, but on the school playground! I never knew the meaning of most of them, but I did once, thinking I was being quite clever, present one to the brother of my close friend. He, being several years older and "in the know," told me sternly I must never use that word again. I still don't know what it meant, but I think I now have a pretty fair inkling.

But as for Pidgin, there was no way to put a stop to that should our parents have wanted to. I have no idea how we picked it up. I think it just seeped into our blood streams.

Pidgin!

"I no savee how makee do this."

"You tellee me no can go."

"You no talkee lonsense. I talkee you momma slappee you face." Our Amah would say to my sister and me. But we both knew how safe we were, because Amah would never report any of our wrong doings to anyone. But no wonder Pidgin was so much a part of growing up in China.

When we were babies in Soochow, we each had our own Amah, Amah Cho Mei and Amah Lo Chi.

"When we left Soochow to go on home leave," Mother told us, "you had to be forcibly taken from the arms of your Amahs. They were both sobbing uncontrollably."

Our Amahs knew they would never see us again. When we returned, we would be taken to another city. We had left Soochow and Amah Cho Mei and Amah Lo Chi forever. When we returned to China, it would be to the city of Tsinan.

CHAPTER II

Tsinan
Love Affairs, No Kindergarten, And Warlords

My memories of Tsinan come mostly as well from small, faded snapshots. As a result, everything in my mind colors Tsinan grey. But then I believe many things actually were. The large house we shared with Standard Oil bachelors, our family occupying the top floor of the building, was grey stucco. The house was a compound of other grey stucco houses, all enclosed by a grey stucco wall. There must have been sunshine in Tsinan. I just don't remember it. But then I was only two when we arrived there, and not quite five when we left.

One of the pictures we have is of a birthday party, either mine or my sister's, and Mother had had it tinted. Therefore it reminds me that there was something not grey in Tsinan, my pink organdy dress, and my sister's lavender, both with little embroidered flowers around the yokes. In that picture as well is one little boy, Peter, whose family lived in our same compound, we both thought terribly spoiled.

"His father," our mother informed us, "brings him a present every day." Every day, mind you! One of our pictures is of the three of us sitting in a rickshaw. In it, he looks a perfectly nice little boy in his Little Lord Fauntleroy suit. But a present every day? Well!

I idolized my sister, despite battles royal over toys, especially at Christmas. One particular memorable battle arose when one Christmas, in what I consider total lack of parental wisdom, we were given one Steiff teddy bear, one mama doll in a lovely pink dress with black velveteen trim, and one doll carriage. These were to be shared.

What were our parents thinking? My sister, bigger and stronger, also future tomboy and my heroine, guardian and protector, managed that whole Christmas day to gain control of the carriage with the doll and teddy bear in it. I spent a great deal of the day chasing after her in tears.

An attempt in Tsinan was made to connect me with the little kindergarten that my sister Connie attended. But that's only hearsay, as I don't remember anything about it. Small wonder. All I did was report at home what my sister had done there. I had done nothing myself but cry when they tried to lead me away from her. It almost goes without saying that I was soon removed from kindergarten.

Tsinan was where I believe I first started falling in love, which always seemed remarkably easy for me to do. There, it was with the young Standard Oil bachelors who lived beneath us. I wasn't fussy. I was in love with all of them, and whenever one came upstairs and sat visiting in the living room, there was I climbing up on his lap. One with a great sense of humor one day stood me on my head in the bathtub with the water running. I thought this was great fun, although Mother did not when she arrived on the scene. I saw nothing wrong. After all, it wasn't as if the plug was in the tub.

But I think the one memory I had of Tsinan that stands out from all the rest is of Coolie coming into the living room almost before the door clicked behind Mother and Father just about every time they went out for the evening. I was always there, too, perched on the sofa, watching him wind up our Victrola and put on his favorite record. Then the two of us, I on the sofa and Coolie standing reverently in front of the Victrola, listened first to "Hey diddle diddle, the cat and the fiddle" followed by "No matter how young the prune may be, he's always full of wrinkles."

What was going on outside our compound I was too small to know or care about. I somehow once remember seeing flashes of light in the sky, and hearing crackling sounds.

"Is it firecrackers?" my sister and I asked. We were just old enough to know about those at least, and we did hear the pop-pop-pop of those strings of tiny red firecrackers, so big a part of Chinese New Year's.

"No, not firecrackers," said Father. "It's the warlords at each other."

Back then warlords ruled in China, and it seemed one was always at war with another. I had no idea what a warlord was, but as it didn't influence my life in any way, such as sending me back to the dreaded kindergarten, I hardly needed to worry about it.

"Daddy and I were once invited to a banquet hosted by the fierce warlord who ruled over the part of China around Tsinan," Mother told us. "This particular warlord's lady friend was apparently very interested in Daddy, and was taking no pains to hide her feelings at the banquet. We were both terrified at what the warlord might decide to do about this. He did nothing, as it happily turned out. He must have been in a good mood that night," Mother said.

But then in the middle of one night, Mother and Father awakened my sister and me, and told us we must get dressed.

"Why?" we asked, both of us frightened.

"A warlord is attacking Tsinan," Father told us.

Could it have been the same one who had had them to the banquet? Was he coming after Father after all?

That was something I never would know. We were taken to the train station, and escaped by train to Tsingtao. We left from there for our home leave to America, and never did return to Tsinan.

That is how China's history came touching our lives back then. It came even closer on our family's next station, and closer still after the following one.

But what was of far more importance to me, was that on that next home-leave to America, when I was five, it was decided once again to attempt to connect me with kindergarten. There was a little girl in my class whose straight dark hair cut in precise bangs across her forehead I can still clearly remember.

It seemed that her primary interest in kindergarten once I arrived was attaching herself to me. She immediately made it her life's work to steal my graham crackers and milk, and box my ears whenever the teacher wasn't looking. So once again, I spent my time crying, and was yanked from that kindergarten as well. It began to look as if I would never get any education at all.

I finally did at our next station, Hankow, the city by the yellow, muddy waters of the fabled Yangtze River.

CHAPTER III

Hankow
The Ching Ming, Summers, And A Leather Slipper

It has always seemed to me that the glamorous, even though muddy yellow, Yangtze River should be the one flowing by the glamorous city of Shanghai instead of a river by the name of Huangpu, although the Huangpu does at least connect with the Yangtze.

This, though, is only a thought I had later. I'm not certain that, at five, or even six and seven, I was especially even aware of the Yangtze flowing only one long block from where we lived, though we could actually see it from the front windows of our apartment in the Ching Ming building.

Our family did have a beautiful apartment covering the whole fourth floor at the top of the building that we rode up to in a splendid wrought-iron elevator. Only the roof garden . . . and it was an actual, grass-covered garden . . . was over us. I don't know yet how our family ever fell heir to that apartment, as it was normally reserved for the head of the Hankow branch of SOCONY. I suspect he and his family must have preferred to have a house rather than an apartment. Louise, their youngest daughter, and I played together at school or at the Hankow Country Club playground, but I never thought to ask her. Who does think of such things at the age of five or six?

But the apartment really was spectacular, with oak parquet floors throughout, and every room enormous, from the living room, the den, the glass-enclosed porch, the dining room, all the way to the bedrooms. Even Mother and Father's bathroom with the old-fashioned toilet tank and chain high up on the wall, and claw-foot tub was grand. Could one have actually skated in Mother and Father's bathroom? I've wondered. Perhaps it wasn't as big as it seemed to me at five.

Well, at least "We once had twenty couples dancing in the living room, with no furniture removed!" Mother said.

But I can only imagine all the sliding and gliding around and doing the Charleston to Yes, Sir, That's My Baby on those gleaming parquet floors, as my sister and I would long since have been sent to bed.

Of course there were parties for us too. I remember one particularly enormous one for me when I turned six, with at least twenty-four young guests, most of whom I didn't even know. That's because they were the children of Father's business associates Mother felt obliged to invite. Birthday games with prizes were followed by everyone seated at table in the huge dining room, opened to its fullest, and complete with balloons, snappers, and table favors. And then, of course, there were the piles of presents for me that I was required to open with everyone staring at me while I did.

I hated it all. I did not wish to have the party. I did not wish a pile of games, puzzles, and books from children I did not know. All I wanted, but never knew how to say so, was a special gift from my mother and father, something like a little gold locket with their pictures in it, or even my own little wristwatch that I could tell everyone proudly was a gift from Mummy and Daddy.

I wonder now at all the things I felt or did not feel, wanted or did not want, and could never bring myself to tell anyone.

****

Summers by the Yangtze were murderously hot and steamy. Ceiling fans did nothing but stir up a few half-dead flies. They certainly did nothing much to cool the stifling air. Sometimes, my sister and I would try to cool off by taking turns wrapping ourselves in a towel, and lowering ourselves into our bathtub filled with cold water.

The only problem with this great plan was that for some reason we had to share one towel, and my heroine sister, being the older, always had her turn first. Therefore I had to wrap a cold, soaking wet towel around myself before entering the tub. I always had to sit on the plug end as well. I wonder why it never occurred to me to complain about this highly inequitable arrangement, but I never did. I can only suppose it was because my sister had convinced me that age has its privileges. It certainly did in her case!

Often at night, our family and several others in the Ching Ming escaped to the roof garden with their camp cots. But the distant rumbling of thunder would send everyone scurrying back downstairs. I truthfully don't remember a single night where we all remained on the roof garden until dawn broke.

"One night it was so bad," Mother was to tell me years later, "that we could no longer take sitting in the apartment listening to rats chasing around the living-room molding, so we escaped to the Country Club."

"Leaving us behind?" I asked, shocked. "Well, you were both sound asleep," explained Mother lamely. "And Amah was there to watch over you."

Amah or no Amah, and sound asleep we may have been, but no doubt dripping wet with rats running around. And the Ching Ming, for all its splendor, did have some magnificent specimens of Yangtze River rats occupying the building along with us.

Did our parents have no guilt sitting and sipping tall, cool drinks on the Country Club lawn, mosquitoes warded off by punk coils twinkling cheerily under the table, leaving us at home with sweating little bodies and rats scurrying around over our heads? Apparently not. At least not back then.

One summer, however, it was decided that Mother, my sister and I, later joined by my father, would escape a Hankow summer by going to Kuling. This was a breathtakingly lovely mountain resort that could only be reached by first taking a riverboat up the Yangtze River to the city of Kiukiang, and then up the mountain by sedan chairs, their bamboo shafts carried by coolies, one in front, one behind.

Mother chose to walk up the path, but my sister and I were each carried in a separate sedan chair. The paths were narrow, steep, rocky, and altogether frightening. When the coolies rounded a hairpin turn, one's sedan chair could swing right over . . . nothing. Nothing but air for miles straight downward. Curiously, I who in Tsinan once woke to find myself upright in bed one night, and sat crying for Amah because I was too frightened to lie back down again, was not one bit frightened at being swung out over a straight fall to the terrifying bottom of a mountain. I can only think it was a child of China's one hundred percent faith in the coolies carrying her, just as she knew that their own Coolie, or Boy, or Amah, would protect her, no matter what.

But in Kuling there were no hot, sticky nights, and no rats running around behind the moldings on the ceiling. Just long, cool days, and instead of the steaming, muddy river, there were sparkling clear streams running by the packed dirt roadways, sometimes collecting in rocky pools for us to splash and swim in.

The only worrisome thing in Kuling was snakes. When our father came up to join us, and we went for walks with him, he always carried a walking cane with a sharp blade at the end. I once saw a snake that was over three frightening feet long and an electric blue-green color . . . the color a dragon might be. Fortunately, he was draped over a bamboo pole, lifeless as the pole itself, but bringing a cold shiver all the same.

We only went to Kuling once, though, and the rest of the summers were endured in steaming hot Hankow. Winters were mild, but sometimes we were lucky enough to have snow. One such winter was the most memorable, because all the servants in the Ching Ming got together to build an enormous snow Buddha in the garden behind the building. When it was completed, they first tinted with red what looked like crabapples he held in his hand. Then they poured water over him, and he became a mountain of glistening ice. Naturally we had to try climbing on what lap he had, but the ice Buddha would have none of it, and off we slid. Thump!

But Hankow was more to me than just hot summers, nights on the roof garden of the Ching Ming building, trips to the Country Club playground, an ice Buddha in the garden, and the Yangtze River two blocks away. Hankow was where I finally embarked again on kindergarten, and actually did not disgrace myself by having to be removed in tears.

But I remember very clearly one tearful session I had that had nothing to do with school. It happened one day when a SOCONY bachelor came to have tiffin, or noontime meal, with us. For some reason my sister and I were included in the event, so sat at the table with the grownups. Linc, the young man, was very nice, but I have to note that I was not in love with him. After all, even at that age, I was discriminating, and did not fall in love with every SOCONY bachelor. I had no romantic interest in red hair, a pink complexion to go with it, and a tiny red mustache. I relate all this by way of explaining that what happened had nothing to do with love.

It started when nearing the end of the meal I had the misfortune to burp.

"Say 'excuse me'," said my father. I didn't.

"You will please say 'excuse me'," said my father.

I hung my head, and said nothing.

The problem was that I found it difficult when I was five and six, make that impossible, to say "how do you do," or "thank you very much," or "excuse me, please." This is one more thing that I could never confess to anyone. How was I to explain it? I don't believe there really is an explanation, so how could I have come up with one? All I know was that I was in misery if called upon to say any of those ordinary little polite phrases.

We ended up in my parents' bedroom, my father sitting on Mother's bench in front of her dressing table, with his brown leather slipper in hand, and me in front of him sobbing, and gulping down tears. He continued telling me to say it, and threatening to spank me if I did not. At last, and it was a very long last, I finally choked out the words "excuse me," or at least a reasonable facsimile of the same. I know my father was happy to accept anything at all.

I've sometimes thought if the scene could be played again, I would never, never, never say it. The thing is that my father (who incidentally was known as the Bobby Jones of China) had never hit anything other than a golf ball. Striking me would have hurt him far more than me, as I know I would have had nothing more than a couple of gentle taps on my rear end. But this would have meant that I had won.

However, this is a very grown-up thought, and how could I have been expected to know it at six? Maybe I'm glad I didn't. I had no reason for wanting to hurt my gentle father any more than he would have wanted to hurt me.

CHAPTER IV

Hankow Continued British School Rules, Riots And Witch Hunts

Because the Hankow British School had closed down even before we arrived due to the riots and unrest in the city, my sister and I were enrolled in a convent school run by French Catholic nuns. Sitting behind me was my best friend, Bradley. He and his brother, George, along with their mother and father, who was also with SOCONY, lived two floors below us in the Ching Ming.

George was my sister's age, and the four of us played tag, and Going Around the Mulberry Bush, and Go In and Out the Window, and just general chasing each other around on the roof garden. Bradley hosted teddy bear teas for me with a tiny tea set and their family "specialty," which I'd never had before, toasted soybean nuts. Toasted soybean nuts forever after have reminded me of those thrilling teddy bear teas.

My gullible sister and equally gullible me, admired the boys greatly, and absolutely believed everything they told us.

"Our apartment is much better than yours," they assured us, even thought their apartment hardly compared to our grand one on the fourth floor.

"We have a much better car than yours," they said, convincing us that their family's Ford was vastly superior to our family's far more expensive Buick. I suppose if they had told us the moon was made of green cheese, we would have believed that as well.

Bradley and I spent a great deal of time having conversations with each other in the classroom. But one day the very nice nun who was our teacher announced, "For the next ten minutes, you will all do nothing but talk to one another." The whole class became tongue tied, and naturally, try though I might, I could not think of a single thing to say to Bradley, nor could he think of anything to say to me. We all sat there through a very uncomfortable ten minutes of silence. Perhaps that nun was cleverer than we supposed!

When the Hankow British School finally reopened, it was as the Hankow British American Private School. The emphasis, though, was on the "British." So there I went every day in my very proper British uniform, a navy blue blazer with the school emblem embroidered in gold thread on the pocket, and under it a Viyella blouse with a prim Peter Pan collar.

There I graduated from the third level kindergarten to first form, where I had to tangle with pounds, shillings, and pence. Twelve pence made a shilling. Twenty shillings made a pound. Nothing nice and simple like one hundred cents to the dollar.

I somehow managed that, and I even played a creditable emissary in the British school play, DICK WHITTINGTON, in which, along with young Dick himself, my sister starred as the Lord Mayor's daughter. But in order to qualify for Brownie, which eventually led to becoming a Girl Guide, the British version of a Girl Scout, I had to draw a British flag as well as the American flag. I would never know if I could have mastered the American flag, because I never made it past the impossibly difficult (or so I thought) British flag. All those uneven spaces between those angled lines. I couldn't figure them out, much less draw them.

Another thing I could not master was use of my right hand. This seemed especially not to please the Hankow British American Private School.

"She must stay every day after school to learn to write with her right hand," Mrs. Rattenbury, the principal, decreed.

So I stayed every day after school to copy again with my right hand everything I had done during the day with my left. This had the effect of making me so pale, peaked, and nervous that Mother looked into it. A note from our doctor soon put a stop to any further attempts by the School to improve my life by instructing me in the use of the very correct right hand.

But I, along with my sister, somehow managed with my incorrect left hand to win all prizes given for examinations and year-end grades. We were given only one each, however.

"It would be unfair for them to walk off with all the prizes," Mrs. Rattenbury and the School decreed.

Unfair to whom? I believe I should have been given an extra prize for finally giving up crying in school, and not having to be escorted from the school in ignominy, taking my offending left hand with me.

Warlords in Tsinan, though, had nothing on the political situation we faced in Hankow. In Tsinan, the warlords were away in the distance somewhere, shooting off fireworks at each other. But for the occasional pop-pop-popping and the glow in the sky, it did not affect us at all. In Hankow, we looked out our windows, and saw fierce rioting around the enormous factory that fronted the river one block away. We saw men pounding and bloodying one another with wooden clubs and bamboo poles. There were some days when we could not even leave the Ching Ming building in safety, and were kept home from school. Father could not even get to his office. But worse than the riots was what was happening in the streets.

That was the time when General Chiang K'ai-shek had parted company with the communists, and was on a communist "witch hunt." Once, as my sister and I were riding in our car with our parents, Mother said, "Both of you, duck your heads down and keep them down."

This was to keep us from seeing the terrible sight of street beheadings. Chinese were simply caught randomly on the street, made to kneel and lay their heads down on boxes to be summarily beheaded. Bits of paper were then dipped in the blood and thrown into the air "to get rid of the devil" and, of course, to serve as a warning to everyone within sight.

The question arises as to how I knew what it was we were not supposed to see if my head was dutifully ducked. Well, my heroine, guardian sister, who it turned up was not as dutiful as I was, peeked, and could hardly wait to report it all to me later. In great gory detail, naturally!

Then one night, Boy, his face frozen with terror, came into the living room to talk to Father. "Dossofoo in jail," he said. "He need dollars to get out."

Dossofoo, it appeared, had been one of those picked up randomly in the street. He would only be released if palms were crossed generously with dollars. Father lost no time in providing Boy with the dollars. If he had not, Dossofoo, an innocent victim, would have been beheaded the next morning.

CHAPTER V

Hankow
Home Leave, A King, A Patsy Ann Doll, And An Indian Giving Lesson

I was eight when we left Hankow, old enough by then to be fully aware of what our home leave, a trip to America, meant. We would sail on the elegant Empress of Japan. I was fascinated by the thought of a journey across the ocean on this great ship. We had a brochure, printed only in brown and white, but every afternoon when I had to take my required "nap," I poured over it in bed, feeling a delicious tingle all over as I studied over and over pictures of the cabins, the dining room, the grand parlor, and elaborate stairs leading from one deck to the next. I read the ink right off the pages of that brochure.

The ship was grand enough for a king, and an actual king was on that ship. He was Prajadhipok, King of Siam, whose grandfather, King Mongkut was the model for the king in the play, Anna and the King of Siam. In Japan, we went from Yokohama to visit Kamakura, and there saw King Pradjadipok burn incense before the Great

Buddha, Daibutsu.

The Empress of Japan took us not to San Francisco, where all our other ships docked, but to Vancouver, Canada. From there we went by train to New York. As California was where we always spent our entire home leaves with Grandma Brooks and our Brooks aunts and uncles, I don't remember why it was that this time we detoured via New York. Perhaps my Father wanted to visit the home office of SOCONY. At eight, I wasn't even curious enough to ask. Why would I? As far as I was concerned, there was one and only one reason for us to go to New York. That was so that we could go to a big department store and buy my heroine sister Connie her beloved Patsy Ann doll. I got a lesser doll and was perfectly happy with it. I suppose I didn't believe I was worthy of having a real Patsy Ann.

When we returned to California, we stayed in an apartment in Santa Barbara on Bath Street. It was just a few blocks away from Grandma Brooks' bungalow, and what I remember most about that is not only the bright pink hibiscus bushes in front, but the wonder we had never experienced in China of picking and eating figs and peaches right from the trees in a back yard. Along with this memory is always the picture of Grandma Brooks wiping her hands on her eternal apron, and saying, "Land sakes! Look at this!" as she picked a fat green worm off her cucumbers or tomatoes in her vegetable garden.

That summer we played with two neighbor girls whose father was an out-of-work carpenter. We must have seemed very rich to them, especially when we were given two dollars, a small fortune back then, to spend any way we chose. We all marched down to the ice cream parlor and spent the whole two dollars on candy and ice cream cones. I wonder what their parents must have thought when they heard about us and our grand two dollars. Peter in his Little Lord Fauntleroy suit, indeed!

The younger of the two girls was Marilyn, my friend. In a burst of generosity one day, just before we were ready to leave Santa Barbara, I grandly gave her my Peter Rabbit box of paints. Then I had a fit of remorse and decided I wanted the box of paints back. I wanted it more than anything in the world.

Marilyn and I had both collected sacks of pebbles in a dried streambed that summer, so I marched over to her house with my sack. She arrived at the door with the paint box.

"You can have my pebbles," I said.

"Oh!" said Marilyn. She was surprised and happy. Here I was with another gift for her.

"You can have my pebbles," I said again, "if I can have my paints back."

"I want to keep the paints," said Marilyn. "I don't want any more pebbles."

"I want my paints back anyway," I said. "Here!" I shoved the sack of pebbles into her hand, grabbed the box of Peter Rabbit paints, and ran home.

Marilyn, her sister, and two other friends all appeared at our door before we left.

"Indian giver!" said her sister. The two friends nodded and looked very solemn and stone faced. Guilty as charged!

I should have given the paint set back to Marilyn. I think I wanted to, but at only eight, didn't know how to go about it. When we left there, I left the box of paints behind in the empty apartment. I never knew if anyone ever found it. All I knew was that I didn't want it anymore.

When we left Santa Barbara, it was go to our next station. Along with Soochow, it was another city that was happily not marked by some sort of political or military unrest replete with fireworks in the sky, riots in factories, or bloody beheadings in the streets. It was a city by yet another river, although still not the Yangtze. It was the River Hai, and the city was Tientsin.

CHAPTER VI

Tientsin, No. 1 Newchwang Loo Stairs, Weddings, A Funeral, And A Vampire Remedy

The fact that Tientsin was once "a vibrant, walled city" when Shanghai was "only a small town in the paddies along the Huang Pu River" would not have meant much to me when we arrived there, if anyone had chosen to inform me about this. I was only interested in the things that immediately affected my eight-year- old self. Furthermore, the fact that I was in China was nothing remarkable to me. I had been born there, and but for home leaves to America, grew up there.

But Tientsin was where I would go from eight to twelve years old, where I would be living in a house instead of an apartment, where I would spend summers in the most glorious summer resort any child could hope for, where I would be in love once more, where I would be going to an American school that did not include pound, shillings, and pence, a complicated British flag to draw, where, most hopefully, the school believed that a left hand was just as good as a right, and where if I were to win two prizes, would actually see that I got them.

However, before we were to be entered in the Tientsin American School, we had a brief stay at the Court Hotel. It is the first thing I remember about the city, the two large stone Foo Dogs, their scowling faces fiercely guarding a long covered passageway with a tiled roof supported by bright red lacquer pillars, that led to the hotel lobby. China personified!

There is one thing, though, that I remember most about our stay at the hotel which had nothing to do with the hotel, with thoughts of school, or even with China itself. It had to do with an American movie my sister had somehow found out about.

"Please can't we go see it?" she teased. And teased. And teased.

"We can't leave Bobbie alone in the hotel," said Mother. "We have no amah yet to leave her with, so, no, we can't go."

"Why can't she come with us?" asked my sister.

Mother apparently couldn't think of a good argument for this, so she decided to take my sister to see The Cat Creeps, and I was dragged along with them.

The Cat Creeps! How could Mother not have guessed what this was all about? The movie featured a sinister mansion draped in shadows, scary music, a ramrod-stiff dead body falling from behind a sliding panel, and most frightening of all, preceding the falling body, a hand slithering out from the same panel to lift a necklace from the neck of the sleeping heroine.

For me, nothing, not even heads rolling in the streets held terrors to match this movie. I spent the better part of it crouching on the floor behind the seat in front of me, and from then on spent nights hiding with my head under the blanket in the room I shared with my sister across the hotel hall from our mother and father.

Every night Father would come in and tell me to bring my head up from under the blanket. "You're going to suffocate if you don't," he said sternly every time.

This turned out to be another one of those things I couldn't tell anyone about. Perhaps someone would have suggested the simple solution of a nightlight. Instead, out would come my head, but only to go back under the blanket the moment Father left the room.

I was filled with envy at my heroine sister bravely sleeping with her head on the pillow. It was only after we were thoroughly grown up that she told me how frightened she had been lying in the dark in our hotel room, though apparently not frightened enough to suffocate herself under a blanket.

It was not until the following summer, when I slept under a mosquito net in the middle of a veranda with no wall behind me to accommodate a terrifying, deadly hand, that under the blanket.

But that was some months later. In the meantime we had left the Court Hotel and moved into the house at No. 1 Newchwang Loo, in the former German concession, the house that would be ours for the next four years.

The two-story red brick house, sitting right on the corner, was almost twice the size of the one where I had first put in an appearance in Soochow. I thought it the most wonderful house, the one I would always remember as the house. Our apartment in the Ching Ming in Hankow was certainly lovely, and could even have been called glamorous, considering that it not only covered a whole floor of the building, but was a fourth-floor penthouse. But it did not have something the house had, and that was stairs!

I suppose we must have had stairs in the Soochow house considering the fact that I was born upstairs, but I wasn't even at the crawling stages when we left, so don't remember stairs any more than anything else about that house. But I was going on nine when we moved to our Tientsin house, and those stairs became an important part of my life.

Stairs! Imagine being able to run up and down stairs! Imagine being able to perch on the top stair, knees drawn up to my chin, and peek through the railings at grown-up parties going on in the large living room below! Ah, to get a first magical look at our Christmas tree, ceiling high and perfectly shaped! "Santa Claus" had come during the night and heaped presents under it. Just before we were allowed to come down, Shao, our Boy, Coolie, and even Dossofoo, would light the hundreds of colored, twisted candles fastened to the branches with little shiny crimped-tin holders. The candles could only be lit that once, and never, ever again, but the sight of them would be remembered forever. The tree was ablaze with their light, and the smell of hot wax mingled with the pungent smell of the freshly cut pine tree. How could electric lights, even though they stay on a Christmas tree until it grows dry and comes down, compete with that?

The only time I didn't care much for the stairs was when I was carried, bumping and thumping, down them in a stretcher, en route to the isolation hospital because I had come down with scarlet fever. I have to admit, though, by then nine-years-old, I probably didn't mind being the star of such a dramatic exit from our house.

In the daytimes, from those stairs, we could look down across the lovely large living room, flanked by a wide opening to the dining room on one side, and a den with a fireplace on the other, right through tall French doors to our brick-walled garden. We could see the brick path leading to a pergola that in spring was a corners of the garden would be ablaze with the yellow of forsythia and fragrant with the blossoms of pale lavender and white lilacs.

Our earlier homes had pretty much been SOCONY furnished as a stay at each station was for no more than three years, and only later extended to four. "Early basic bleak" is what I can remember of it even in our elegant Ching Ming apartment. Our Tientsin house was completely unfurnished, and the first one Mother had a free hand in decorating entirely herself. What she accomplished was remarkable, considering that we were not the wealthy people friends and relatives in America seemed to think we were.

But who could have guessed it from the furnishings in our house? Almost all the furniture came from Sims, an English furniture maker in China, built and carved by Chinese craftsmen. Every room had one or more custom designed, handmade Chinese rugs from the Nichols Rug Factory in Tientsin.

The curved backs of twelve gleaming mahogany dining room chairs were carved in a delicate Queen Anne design. Our living room furniture was upholstered in cream-colored brocades, with rich brown velvet seats. A handsome carved rosewood dragon floor lamp stood guard in a corner. Down filled pillows in den chairs were covered in deep blue cut velvet.

Carved rosewood nested tables and coffee tables were the wonderful Chinese accents.

Upstairs was an all-pale-blue master bedroom. The exotic guest room was furnished with a rose, silk-covered headboard, and a black rug in the "broken basket" pattern of rose, gold, and lavender chrysanthemums splashed over it. Besides our playroom, my sister and I had a dainty pink bedroom. The rose silk and lace cover of a kidney-shaped table Mother would one day temporarily borrow to make into a costume for my sister when she and her friend Bonnie danced a minuet at an American community's celebration of George Washington's birthday.

I think this last says more than anything about our mother's cleverness and artistry in furnishing the house. Everything in the house was made in China, and contrary to what anyone might think, at far less cost than anything imported from another country. Furthermore, that rosewood carved dragon that stood watch over the living room was something she proudly purchased from her winnings at mah-jongg.

Our servants had their quarters in the basement.

"It's their home," we were told by our parents. "You're not go down and bother them there."

This was largely directed at me, as I was the one who spent so much time haunting the kitchen. But Dossofoo in the kitchen was one thing. In his home in the basement was quite another. I did often wish I could go down there at Chinese New Year's when, according to Chinese custom, they spent the better part of the night making and steaming bau jaudzes, the traditional dumplings of meat wrapped in dough. I didn't think it fair that I couldn't be in on this. Why would just watching hurt anything? I told myself I didn't think Dossofoo would mind. But I never dared risk it.

What went on in our own house, though, was all I would ever

know of any house on our street. The word "neighborhood" did not apply. I never knew who lived next door to us in an equally large house. And I positively never knew who lived across the street, or what was going on there. Neither did any of us except our servants, who in some mysterious way seemed to have an invisible pipeline to everything going on both in and outside that house.

The house across the street was enormous. It was at least twice as big, if not far bigger, than ours. "Mansion" was a word more aptly fitted to it than just plain "house." It was a great grey building guarded by a forbidding high grey wall. A gateman kept a twenty-four watch beside a double black iron-barred gate.

What we believed was that an enormously wealthy Chinese family lived there. We believed this not only from the size of the building, the high wall, the gateman guarding it, but mostly from Dossofoo, who seemed to have a special pipeline to everything going on around us, and was happy to pass on the servants' gossip.

"People live there very rich," he said. "Very, very rich," he repeated to make sure the message was not lost.

I got in on many of these pieces of news because I spent a great deal of time haunting the kitchen, getting under Dossofoo's foot as he chopped vegetables on the kitchen table, or pulled a cake from the oven of our great black iron coal-burning stove.

"Shao kuei!" Dossofoo called me. Little Devil! Boy and Coolie referred to me as that as well. But it wasn't meant in the same way foreigners were referred to as "foreign devils." It was more a term of affection. Or maybe not always, because after all, I really was a little pest, hanging around and getting in Dossofoo's way.

Dossofoo's further observations included what was going on in the house across the street. "Somebody in house getting married," he said. "Big wedding. Big, big wedding!"

With this announcement, we were prepared for the wedding procession. And it was the size and splendor of the processions that started at the house to snake their way around the city, which confirmed what Dossofoo had said in the "very, very rich" matter. An ornate large wedding chair lavishly decorated with gold. Behind it was an ear- splitting loud band of Chinese musicians. Dozens of family relatives and wedding guests, dressed in electric pinks, reds, shimmering peacock blues and emerald greens, trailed behind the band in a cheerful, noisy parade.

Within the wedding chair, mysteriously hidden behind heavy curtains, sat the bride. If old tradition held, and it most likely did then, her wedding would have been arranged by a go- between. The bride would soon see her bridegroom for the very first time, someone with whom she must spend the rest of her life.

This last is something I didn't know back then. It seems curious that it never occurred to me even to ask about it or wonder about any of it. But then after all, I was probably too young to think about those things. Besides, I had grown up in China, and thus had grown up seeing many of such wedding processions. They were simply there, simply part of the scenery. I would no more have thought of asking questions about them than asking why there were clouds in the sky.

Once Dossofoo said, "Somebody in house die. Big funeral. Big, big funeral."

It was big . . . actually . . . huge. It also advertised the family's great wealth, and was equally as impressive as the weddings. It featured a coffin that was elaborately draped and decorated, and large and heavy enough to need several men to carry it. Behind came not only the dozens of relatives and guests, but men waving rods of feathery, make-believe "tears." In addition to these were the white-robed professional mourners who were paid to wail day and night outside the house, and wailed with equal fervor in the procession.

In addition to the procession, an enormous feast was prepared in the empty field across the street.

"They make food for poor people," I was informed by Dossofoo. "Big bribe to make sure he get to heaven."

It didn't seem to matter that the cheerful multitudes showing up might be something other than "the poor," for a bribe this large to the gods would most certainly insure a smooth passage into heaven for the recently departed.

"Plenty paper money, animals, food, and clothes get burned to see he have comfortable passage to other world," Dossofoo said.

The funeral I remember took place in a hot September. The pungent smells of oil and soy sauce, and meat cooking in large steaming cauldrons wafted across the street. They were accompanied by the continuous wailing of funeral horns and the professional mourners. Night seemed to enhance the sounds and the smells. What had been bearable during the day, became unbearable for me one night. The grim sounds became terrifying, and the thick smells became nauseating.

Lying in bed, I tried to shut it all out, and fall asleep. Instead I became violently sick to my stomach. I was still just as I had been when I was born, a puny child, thin, now become anemic, terribly underweight, and sensitive. It actually never took much to have me losing a meal, which I did as regularly as clockwork. My sister was used to this kind of performance on my part. But on that night, I became so ill I frightened her. She did something never tried before. She tracked our mother and father down at a Country Club party to summon them home.

Mentioning this latter along with the escape from the Ching Ming rats might make it look as if we were constantly being abandoned by our parents, leaving us in dire situations. But that wasn't the case at all. A busy social life often centered around a country club was hardly unique to our parents. It was a way of life in China back then. We thought no more of it than we did Mother playing mah-jongg in the mornings or afternoons, or Father playing golf. We were always watched over and guarded by trusted servants. Never for a moment did we ever feel deprived or abandoned.

At any rate, I loved hanging around Mother's dressing table, watching her get ready for a dance at the Club. I was fascinated watching her dab her nose with Coty powder from the round orange box decorated with powder puffs that looked like large bunny tails with stems. Then finally came the dabbing behind the ears of Quelques Fleurs from its enchanting little perfume bottle. I smelled both fragrances again, deliciously mingled when she gave me a powdery, perfume-y kiss good-night before leaving, all pretty five feet of her on the arms of our handsome six-foot-two- father.

But as for me and my puniness, I had developed full-blown anemia when we came to Tientsin and fortunately was in the care of an excellent English doctor, Dr. Grice. Unfortunately, however, he had me taking some perfectly horrible granulated powder called Ventriculin, made from the gastric tissue of hogs. Hogs, mind you. Not even just pigs! It tasted just as bad as it sounds. Mother also bought a meat press and had Dossofoo squeeze raw beef with it.

"This is meat juice," Mother said, feeding me by the teaspoonful the result of this raw- meat squeezing.

She didn't have to make up a suitable name to persuade me to take it. I thought it was delicious. It never occurred to me until recently that what I had drunk with such relish was blood. The food of vampires!

Mother did indeed have quite a time trying to add a little fat to my skinny bones. Her fattening philosophy included having Dossofoo serve me plates heaped with food, which at breakfast included plates loaded with eggs, toast, and bacon, or bowls filled with mountains of steaming oatmeal. Such piles of food were so daunting one or two bites was all I could get down. Tiny portions the size of a peanut I could have managed, and then proudly joined the "clean plate club." But how was Mother to guess this? For that matter, like all those other things, how did I even know to tell her back then?

Breakfasts were the worst, especially when each year, for at least a week or two after the summer holiday, I would throw up what little I was able to get down on a daily basis before I set out for school. I was a general little wreck anyway, tearfully complaining that I couldn't go to school because as I said each year, starting, for instance, with third grade, "How can I go to third grade. I don't know anything!" "You only don't know what they will be teaching you in third grade," my mother and father kept telling me. "That's why you are going there. You're not expected to know third grade in advance."

What with all that throwing up, blood drinking, and having to have explained what third grade was going to do for me, I often wonder how I survived to grow up.

CHAPTER VII

Tientsin Spit, Smells, China Sounds And School

As soon as we moved into No. 1 Newchwang Loo, we had to start school. Although we had missed several months of school because of our home leave, my sister went right into fifth grade. However, being my by-now full-blown anemic self, Mother decided I had better go into the third grade I hadn't quite finished when we left for America. There was some attempt made to give me extra work so I could catch up and move into fourth. It soon became clear, though, that though my spirit might have been willing, my puny little body was not. So in third grade I remained.

This was particularly sad for me because my friend Bradley, whose family was now also in Tientsin, had progressed to fourth grade. It so happened, though, that he lived only a block from us, so we could play together after school. He often walked home with me, and when we parted company, we faced one another and each backed off one step.

"Good-bye forever!" said Bradley. "Good-bye forever!" I said.

Then we each backed off another step. "Good-bye forever!" said Bradley. "Good-bye forever!" I said.

We kept this ritual up until he was at least half a block away. The two of us really were from the same far-out planet.

The house Bradley and George now lived in was usually reserved for the General Manager of SOCONY. It was quite an enormous house. Curiously, now that where they lived was truly grander than where we lived, they never mentioned it. Besides this house, Bradley and George had also acquired a baby brother by then, John Boy, the little prince of their household. I think that as a result of this, Bradley was always glad to escape his grand home and come play with me at our house. At any rate, what with our understood-only-by-us rituals and games, plus teddy bear teas, I think Bradley was probably the best friend I ever had.

By the time we started school, it was winter.

Stinging winds had started to blow in from the Gobi Desert. They brought with them not only bitter cold, but Gobi Desert dust as well. There was no such thing as storm windows. Shao and Coolie stuffed cotton around the cracks of the windows of the house to keep out the cold and the dust.

I used to watch Coolie piling Tong Shan coal pellets in the den fireplace. They would be glowing and sending off sparks when we came in from school. My sister would imperiously ring for Shao to bring her cocoa and toast, then plop down in front of the fireplace with a book. I usually went first to the kitchen to get my own cocoa and toast, and bother Dossofoo into the bargain, I don't doubt, while he prepared dinner.

"We will have to have coats made for the two of you," Mother said. "I hope I can find a good tailor." And, of course, she did.

I hated having to stand still while a tailor, a row of pins bristling from his mouth, always seemed perilously close to sticking one of them into me as well as the garment I was being pinned into. But there was no such thing as buying clothes in a store, so having clothes made by a Chinese tailor was a fact of life in China. I had to put up with it.

Before we started school, we both had coats made from English camel's hair and fur collars made from Chinese cats. I didn't especially like the idea of a cat providing fur for my collar, but there wasn't fake fur back then, and cat fur was probably free for the taking, as cats were plentiful as wonks, the stray dogs that wandered the streets.

The Tientsin American School was within easy walking distance of our house. Most of the way we traveled along a broad street, Woodrow Wilson Street, a curious name for a street in the German Concession in a Chinese city. But it was actually once named

Kaiserwilhelmstrasse, we were told, and changed by the Chinese after World War I in honor of their American ally.

The street was lined with old acacia trees. On one side were the huge homes of Chinese and foreign families. Opposite them was a large fenced field with buildings in the distance. We were told it was a police station, and that the police drilled on that field. But we never saw them doing it. The field was well kept, but always deserted.

A friend of my sister's lived in one of the big houses on that street. She rode to school in a rickshaw every day, while we walked. "Very, very rich," Dossofoo would have said if he'd known about this. The only reason we had to envy her, though, was on days when the icy cold winds blew in from the Gobi Desert. There she was, her knees all snugly wrapped in a warm plaid blanket in her rickshaw, while we trudged down the street with our chins dug into our cat fur collars.

On the way to school we sometimes passed the street vendors that made the sounds we had awakened to. The sharp clanging of iron plates jerked upward was the special sound of the sharpener of scissors and knives. The clop- clop of pellets striking a gong announced the man who mended broken porcelain. The sounds of China!

The food vendors had their own special sounds, long, drawn-out wails, or short sharp calls like the bark of a dog. Early-rising Chinese businessmen and rickshaw coolies were clustered around them sucking up small meat dumplings or hot steaming noodles into their mouths with chopsticks. On mornings when I hadn't been busy throwing up my breakfast, those noodles were tantalizing. But never, never, would we ever, ever be allowed to eat anything bought from a street vendor. Never! And most especially not in summer. Cholera!

We never stopped being warned about the dreaded cholera.

"Daddy didn't know what to do about it before we were married," Mother told us. "He lived on toast and boiled chicken. He is six foot two inches, and was down to one hundred thirty-five pounds when he came to Shanghai, but at least he never got cholera,"

"He got bit by a mad dog instead," I said cheerfully.

"Not very funny," said Father. "I might have died from that. No, correction, I would have died from that if I'd listened to the doctor who told me not to worry about it. The manager of the SOCONY office told me to take the dog's head to Shanghai. They started me on rabies shots right away, and that's when I met your mother on a blind date."

"I thought you met because she was a nurse," I said.

"That was just a plus," said Father.

Anyway, it was good to know that it was only a mad dog responsible for the arrival into the world of my sister and me, and not the dreaded cholera.

But not being allowed to slurp up delicious hot noodles from the hot noodle man was a minor concern. There were two actually somewhat unpleasant things we had to deal with on the way to school. One was spit.

"Watch out for the spit!"

"Oh, you've gone and stepped right on the spit!"

Spit was another fact of our lives; Chinese men were master spitters. This was not the busiest part of the city. There were few cars, and few rickshaws, and hardly any pedestrians on the sidewalks. But somehow there was always lots of spit. Those little glistening mounds lay there practically inviting someone to step on them.

The other thing we had to deal with was crossing the stone bridge over a narrow creek crowded with sampans. The problem lay in having to stop breathing as we crossed because of the smell. It was bad in the winter. It was unbearable in the summer. Fortunately, it didn't take us long to master the art of avoiding both the spit and the smells. We were not children of China for nothing.

The Tientsin American School itself was a very large brick building that must once have belonged to a wealthy Chinese family. A high, grey concrete wall surrounded a lot in front of the building. It must have been a beautiful garden once, but now was a dusty playground where we played marbles down on our knees, jumped one-legged in games of hop scotch, swung on swings, climbed on money bars, and played baseball on a baseball diamond marked off in the dust.

Beyond the wall at the far end of the playground ran the Hai River. As we played on the swings back there, we could hear the chanting sing-song of coolies laboring under heavy burlap sacks of peanuts and grain, carried from junks tied up to the riverbank.

"Aiya-hoa! Aiya-hoa!" one a background sound mingling with our own sounds we made as we swung and sang at the top of our lungs.

"I see London, I see France, I see somebody's underpants!" and other equally uplifting chants.

We were all children of American businessmen and missionaries, except for the boys and girls whose fathers were with the American 15th Infantry Regiment stationed in Tientsin. They were brought in every day by mule-drawn wagon. None of the rest of us thought there was anything unusual about this. It was simply another fact of life in Tientsin.

Third grade was when I came down with scarlet fever, got carried of to the Isolation Hospital, and missed even more school. But I managed to stick with third grade and not get pushed even further back. Otherwise, school was just school. There are three things, though, that I especially remember about my school days in Tientsin.

One afternoon while still in third grade, just before story time I committed the "crime" of being slow in putting my books and papers away in my desk drawer.

"You are holding up the class," said my teacher.

I had no intention of having my drawer turn into a rat's nest like those the boys had in their into my drawer.

"That's enough," said my teacher. "We're not going to wait any more. You had better go and stand in the hall until story time is over."

Punished for being neat!

The second "crime" was when I ran in from the playground one morning to get my coat from the cloakroom. There stood the principal, Mrs. Payton, and my teacher.

"You're not supposed to be running in and out of the building," said my teacher.

"But I wasn't," I said.

"You mustn't talk back," said Mrs. Payton. Both ladies looked at me with pinched noses and very tight lips.

" I . . . I wasn't," I stammered. "I was only coming in to get my coat."

"That's enough," said my teacher. "I think she had better remain in the playground for five extra minutes after recess tomorrow, don't you, Mrs. Payton?"

Five minutes! A lifetime alone in an empty playground!

The next morning, the minute the bell rang signaling the end of recess, I started counting. I counted as fast I could, finished well before everyone else had entered the building, and ran through the door, breathless. There stood Mrs. Payton and my teacher.

"Weren't you told to stay outside five minutes after recess?" my teacher said.

"Yee, five minutes," I said. "I counted to sixty five times!"

That was five minutes in my mind. It seemed that at nine years old and in the third grade, I had never learned how to tell time!

Mrs. Payton and my teacher exchanged glances, but at least they took pity on me, and I was allowed to stay. Such grave injustices, however, are never forgotten. Perhaps it explains why I remember the names of the principal, my fifth and sixth grade teacher, even the seventh and eighth grade teacher, but not my third and fourth grade teacher. I seem to have blotted her name from my memory entirely.

But one thing I remember most of all from my Tientsin school days was something I can blame on no one but myself. It is one of the things in this world I would most like to be able to do over again. The seed of it, I think, was planted way back in Hankow when I wanted a small gift from "Mummy and Daddy" instead of big birthday parties. I was eleven and in the fifth grade when I came up with the grand idea of exchanging gifts with three other girls in my class.

One of the girls was Dorothy She was about sixteen, a lovely Chinese girl who was only in that grade because for the first time she was learning the English language along with other studies. Her two brothers, John and Paul, were also in the same class, but they were the same age as the rest of us because they had been in the school from the start.

For the gift exchange, I gave Dorothy what to me was a great treasure. Amah had put together two matchboxes to form a tiny doll bed, then covered them with pieces of pale blue velvet left over from Mother and Father's bedroom curtains. She had decorated the bed with a string of tiny pink silk flowers.

Dorothy's gift to me was a pair of dangling jade earrings. It was the finest jade set in gold. Jade and gold earrings in exchange for a doll bed made of matchboxes! I tried to hide my disappointment over earrings I could never wear. She must have done the same with my gift to her. But I had no idea how valuable the earrings might be until I showed them to my mother and father.

"They must be worth a fortune!" my father said.

"Should I give them back?" I asked.

"You can't," said my mother. "She would be terribly insulted. I'm afraid there's not much that can be done about it now."

What made all this worse was that Dorothy had said when she gave me the earrings, "Please, you must not tell my brothers about this. They might tell my father." There was real fear in her eyes.

Once when our very inflammable French teacher, Madame Barrere, was angry with John over work he had done, she threw his notebook on the floor, scattering the pages all across the floor. John burst into tears. He was not concerned about the loss of notebook so much as having to report to his father that he needed another one, and why. The father was very wealthy, and the cost of the notebook was nothing. But John, Paul, and Dorothy were all terrified of him. You may be sure she not only never told him about the earrings, but never showed him the doll bed made of matchboxes!

Even though this exchange of gifts had a different slant to it, it somehow has always brought to my mind O. Henry's Gift of the Magi. Just as I have wished for a different end to that story, I have always wished that there could have been a different ending to mine.

Us in the back garden in Tsinan.

A pair of beauty queens aboard an ocean liner.

BARBARA BROOKS WALLACE

Mother and us off on a rickshaw ride.

Gay Caballero and Snowball at a New Year's ball

CHAPTER VIII

Sisters, Funnies, The Boys, Wonks, And Saturdays

Bonnie (who also rode to school in her own rickshaw and had her own horse besides!), Joyce, Joy, Olive (the daughter of our English piano teacher) . . . all were my sister's good friends.

I had no friends, good or otherwise, except Bradley. Of course, he had other friends as well, and only played with me if he wasn't with them.

It wasn't that I was so unpopular no one wanted to be my friend. It was just that there wasn't much of a pool of girls to draw from. Janet and Luby, who was Russian, were two girls in my same classroom although a grade above me, who were friendly to me, but not "friends," the kind who visited each other's homes after school. They were both considerably more "developed" than skinny, wide-eyed little me. I never knew what they spent so much time whispering to each other about, although I suspected it was "boys."

Now that I think about it, those two girls actually did tease me about Bradley. We were never "boy and girl friend." We were just friends. When we grew up, people were to say that they always thought we would marry. Bradley and I thought this was terribly funny.

"We were always just good friends," we said to each other.

But, "Bradley and Bobbie sitting in a tree K-i-s-s-i-n-g." Sang Jeanette and Luby at the swings.

"Aiya-hoa" sang the coolies carrying their loads of grain and peanuts by the banks of the Hai River, unfortunately not loud enough to drown out the girls.

A girl in my class was in on the gift exchange, but being friends with her was almost impossible. She came on the mule-drawn cart in the morning, and left as soon as school ended in the afternoon.

I liked Dorothy, but she was sixteen, five years old than I was, and from a different world. After school in the afternoon, she scurried home with her brothers.

My sister often brought a friend over after school. Or sometimes Coolie went with a "chit" to their homes to invite them over. They would take their toast and cups of cocoa, disappear into the little bedroom my sister and I shared, and shut the door. Tight!

I was left with the very nice playroom Mother had made for us, complete with a wall- to-wall shelf divided into rooms that were cleverly furnished to look like the rooms of our house, a little doll-sized electric stove, doll cradles and carriages, a shelf full of games. But I was to play in it alone. Once in a while I got brave and knocked on our bedroom door.

"Who is it?" asked my sister. "Me," I replied.

"What is it you want?' she asked.

"Nothing," I had to reply, and then drifted away.

No wonder I spent so much time haunting the kitchen and bothering Dossofoo.

In fairness, my sister, though only a year older than I, was now two grades ahead of me in school. That made a difference in both friends and interests. One thing they were into was movie stars. They poured over the latest PHOTOPLAY, cut out pictures, and invented love stories with paper dolls. I was always thrilled when once in a while they let me hang around and watch.

I was fortunately pretty good at keeping myself entertained as I was left to my own devices so much of the time. I played with my dolls, which I saw to it were always sick and needed my attention. I must have taken after my mother in that respect.

"Tinichka, my beloved only doll was made from an old towel," said Mother, who grew up in a terribly poor family in Russia, "but I saw to it that she always had to be 'sick' so she needed my nursing care."

Mother did graduate from the Harvard Medical School of China in Shanghai to become a nurse. Becoming a nurse was never in my future, but I still kept my dolls in sick bed most of the time, often dressed in some old raggedy shirt of mine. My sister thought this was silly.

It was only one of the things about me she disapproved. Another was that I saved every little thing given to me. This was well and good except that I even saved things that weren't meant to be saved. One I especially remember was a small jar of Bunte raspberry drops. They were raspberry jam encased in a hard candy shell shaped like a raspberry. We got them in our stockings at Christmas. Within two days, hers were all gone.

I never so much as opened mine. Not ever! I don't know what ever happened to them. They remained locked up in their bottle, forever as far as I know, probably turning grey with age, but locked forever in my mind, red, sparkling, and delicious.

My philosophy was that by looking at them, and dreaming over them, I enjoyed them over and over again. My sister's raspberry drops were over and done with in a flash. But naturally she claimed that I never enjoyed them at all. A big difference of opinion, although I expect many people would agree with her. Of course, they would be wrong.

Despite my letting her get away with some of the things she did, like the bathtub dipping arrangement, or even never complaining about having to wear her hand-me-down clothes, which included the coat with the cat fur collar, I suppose she must have somehow resented all the attention that my puny, anemic little self, the "baby" of the family, received.

But I wouldn't have known it, because she never took it out on me. She was a sturdy tomboy who always protected me on the playground if I needed protecting, or when we played with George and Bradley. She really was my heroine when we were growing up.

And despite some developing differences as we grew up, we did share many things together. One I remember had to do with chocolates. At Christmas, Father was always showered with gifts, some rare and valuable, from the Chinese agents. As he had been promoted to an office executive, these agents went out for him to sell "oil for the lamps of China." Among other things, they loved to give boxes of chocolates. Countless boxes of chocolates! For some reason, most of these chocolates were filled with the most terrible synthetic strawberry creams. My sister and I methodically and secretly punched small holes in the bottoms of the chocolates to find ones that were not strawberry creams. Then we carefully laid the rejects back in their little paper cups in the fancy gold and silver-foil-wrapped boxes.

It got worse when SOCONY decided that "rare and valuable"

gifts might appear to be bribes for special favors. Only gifts of food were then allowed. More chocolates! But some years later when my sister and I were in America, Mother and Father reported that they had received thirty turkeys for Christmas! I still wonder if they were alive. I should have asked.

But aside from such things as punching holes in chocolates, and other delights, I still had to find ways to entertain myself on my own. One of my favorite ways was reviewing the little treasures I had in a small two-by-two- foot chest of four rosewood drawers that had been a Christmas present from my parents. Among the treasures were tiny glass animals made in China . . . a pink dragon, tiny frogs and white ducks with yellow bills and black glass dots for eyes. There was a yellow camel and black cat from Germany, and a white crystal bunny and two red goldfish from Japan.

One drawer held a pencil box with a Japanese scene printed on it's sliding top, as the box had come from Japan. It was in two hinged layers, which made it special in my eyes. The box held two pristine Pink Pearl erasers in the top layer, and six new unsharpened Eberhard Faber yellow pencils in the bottom level. I loved to look at these, and would never dream of sharpening the pencils to use them, or use the Pink Pearls to erase anything. They were like Bunte raspberry drops. Just think of those pencils sharpened and worn down! Or the Pink Pearls dirty with their lovely sharp edges rubbed away!

One year I had stored in one drawer a wood pen painted red and a pen painted blue. There was a bottle of blue ink and a bottle of red ink as well to go with the pens. I had bought them one summer, and dreamed over this clever purchase all the way until Christmas when they were to be a gift for my mother and father. It's a wonder I was able to part with them at all, but along with admiring them, I was able to enjoy over and over the act of presenting them, and imagining the joy with which they would be received.

"What a clever gift!" they would say. "Matching pen and ink!"

I don't believe that's what they said at all, but I'd still had the thoughts all those months dreaming about it.

One drawer of my chest also held a little sack of shiny pebbles and a box of seashells I had found. And then there was the small gold tube that might have once held Mother's lipstick. Now it held a tiny roll of paper with a poem on it. This is the poem in its entirety:

"I had a little mouse, Who had a little house Right in the middle of my bedroom. Every time he'd sneeze, I'd give him a piece of cheese."

The author of this splendid poem was me. And just as I reviewed everything else in the drawer, I pulled out the little roll of paper and reviewed the poem over and over. I'm sure I was just as proud of it as all the children's writers I've read about who had their poems and stories published in newspapers or magazines at an impossibly early age.

Besides playing nurse to my dolls, reviewing the treasures in my little chest, and getting under Dossofoo's foot in the kitchen, I read. Or I should say, re-read. Whereas my sister was thought to have read every book in the Tientsin American School library, I mostly read my favorite book, Tiger Tim's Annual over and over. Just as I practically read the print off the Empress of Japan brochure in Hankow, I think I did the same with my Tiger Tim Annuals. I add an "s" to that because a new one came out annually, and it was one of my greatest joys to find it under the Christmas tree each year.

Tiger Tim Annuals were from England, as were the British Girl's Annuals my sister got. Actually, many of our toys as well as books were from England. But one year the big thrill was something ordered from an American catalogue. Mother and ordered one for each of us this time, Toodles dolls. Their bodies were made of rubber, and they actually could have a bath in water. Our dolls until then had cloth or composition bodies.

To be able to give a doll a bath was amazing to us. My growing-up sister was just as excited about it as I was.

Something else also came from America, something we both read avidly. The funnies!

They came from Grandma in Santa Barbara, who saved the Sunday funnies from the Los Angeles Times every week for six months, and then sent the whole lot to us in two or three magical bundles.

We loved Gasoline Alley, Harold Teen, and all the rest. But it was Tarzan of the Apes that we most loved. We could hardly bear to wait to see what happened to Tarzan when we reached the end of our six-months supply. We had to wait another agonizing six months to find out what happened to him next.

"Funnies come!" Shao would tell us with a big grin on his face as soon as we arrived through the front door from school.

Then he had to stand aside as we stampeded into the living room where the bundles would be, waiting for us to tear them open. Then as soon as they were all laid out in proper order, we were down on the floor, lost for hours, reading. The day funnies arrived was unquestionably a day second only to Christmas!

My sister and I and George and Bradley mostly went our separate ways at school, although Bradley and I weren't separate enough apparently for Janet and Luby who thought Bradley was "cute," and enjoyed teasing us. But I didn't have to worry about "Bobbie and Bradley sitting in a tree" kissing or anything else when we played together outside of school. And the four us, George, Bradley, my sister and I still often played together on Saturdays especially, mostly in each other's gardens just as we had on the roof garden of the Ching Ming in Hankow.

The boys lived in an enormous house that was, as our apartment had been in the Ching Ming, actually intended for the Tientsin general manager of SOCONY. The boys never brought this to our attention, though, probably because it was so obvious it wasn't necessary. Their house also had a huge garden, which included an old, dilapidated rickshaw. Bradley would pull it around the garden, but it was so rickety he couldn't get anyone to ride in it. I wasn't the only one who thought it was much too dangerous.

But as far as I was concerned their garden held another hazard, at least for me. Their house held little prince Johnny Boy, but it also included further royalty, two huge great Danes. They were appropriately named King and Queen. They scared me to death, once especially when they jumped on each other playfully, and I was right in the middle, screaming my head off. It was a good thing my heroine sister was there to rescue me.

One of the things we did on weekends in the winters was ice skate. Or at least, some of us did. The boys' garden was so enormous that in winter there was enough room to turn the center bed into an ice rink where we skated on weekends. Not surprisingly, I always stood on the sidelines watching the rest of them gliding around. This wasn't my fault, I see now. I suppose because I always wore hand-me-downs of my sister's, it was thought perfectly fine for me to wear her hand-me-down ice skates. I didn't know I should complain about the fact that my feet rattled around inside the boots to which the skates were attached, not to mention the accompanying pain. I must have thought everyone had the same problem.

Most of the skating, though, was done on the Country Club pond that became an ice rink in winter. There I was at least able to get on the ice because the Club provided chairs with runners that could be pushed around. So with ankles practically horizontal, I was able to stagger around on the ice with the others. On one memorable non-ice-skating Saturday, I was at home for some reason, and my sister was out with the boys. She came into the house excitedly to find me.

"George and Bradley are outside," she said. "And guess what?"

"I don't know, what?" I asked.

"We've got two puppies. We found them in a trench outside the police compound," said my sister. "I'm going to ask if we can keep them."

"Where are they now?" I asked.

"Right outside in the garden. Come see them."

I've always believed that there would never be anything cuter than those two wonk puppies. Patsy was black with brown markings, and Frankie was white with brown ears and tail. They were the sweetest, nicest dogs, and miraculously, we were allowed to keep them. But then Father decided that he wanted to have the dog he had always wanted as a boy. It wasn't any special kind of dog that he'd wanted, just a dog.

But it seemed that wonks were not what he had in mind. He wanted a purebred. There was no way that this purebred could rub noses with our two wonks, or for the matter that the family wanted three dogs. So we were told Patsy and Frankie would have to go. They had by now outgrown cute puppyhood, but we loved them nonetheless. All we had left was Mother's promise that they would find good homes for our puppies. We think they may have gone across the river to the SOCONY storage compound, but we never really knew.

Patsy and Frankie were replaced with Buddy, an Airedale puppy with a proper pedigree. I can't deny it: he too was terribly cute. But Father, for all of having his lifelong wish for a dog fulfilled, didn't know about training him. Neither did the rest of us. So Buddy pretty much ran wild. He ruined our garden by nipping off the buds of every flower ever planted there. In the house he tore around like a lunatic, chewing up everything he could get his teeth around.

Unfortunately, Buddy was also pedigreed. Wonks were legion in China, but pedigreed dogs were rare and highly prized. One summer, Buddy simply disappeared. Father wrote Mother, my sister and me when we were away in Peitaho for our summer holiday. He told us the servants told him Buddy had run away, but Father had every reason to believe he was stolen. Buddy had been responsible for us losing our Patsy and Frankie. He was mischievous and naughty. But we loved him, nonetheless, and were heartbroken.

We never had another dog as long as we lived in China.

There were no more thrilling events like the bringing home of two puppies, but many Saturdays were often special anyway. Those were the times when my sister and I went with George and Bradley to a matinee at the Capitol Theatre, which, like our school, was within walking distance of our homes.

On our journey there, we encountered the same "hazards" with which we'd met on our way to school, the spit and the smells. And sometimes there would be beggars, beggars horribly maimed with stumps where arms or legs should be. Some were not much older than we were. We were told they had been deliberately crippled to look more pitiful. I never grew immune to the sight of these beggars. But they were a sight we had grown up with in the China of then. I could only try not to see them as we walked by them.

Sometime another friend or two would join us on our movie afternoon. What we would probably be seeing was a Tarzan or a Shirley Temple movie. The Chinese people adored Shirley. We did, too. But if push came to shove between Shirley and Tarzan . . . well! We always arrived early, sat in the balcony, and waited for that magical moment when the asbestos with all the ads pasted on it would slowly rise as the house lights dimmed.

It was still bright daylight when we came out, eyes blinking as we stumbled back into the real world. We never went to a movie without immediately afterwards crossing the street to Kiessling & Bader Cafe, the legendary German baker and confectioners. We loved to ogle the petit fours behind the glass counter. Our favorites were the pale green ones in the shape of frogs, with open mouths revealing pink butter cream within, and the mini-mountains of pale chocolate cream coated in dark chocolate frosting and always topped with a silver dragee.

But we only had those when we went to tea with our parents. What we went for after the matinees were the wonderful Kiessling & Bader ice cream cones. It was always a game to see who could make their cone last longest on the way home. I may have been puny and terrible at any outdoor game ever invented that required strength or speed, but I excelled at ice-cream cone licking, which required slowness, delicacy, and determination. I could make mine last past the street where the boys turned off, and all the way to our front door, clearly a winner. This, of course, never impressed my sister. I believe if I think hard enough, I might come up with some analogy between this and the saving of the Bunte Raspberry Drops. "Determination" at least would apply.

These pleasant Saturdays, however, took place only during the school year. In the summers, Mother went with my sister Connie and me to Peitaho, surely the dream vacation place of every child who has ever been there.

CHAPTER IX

Peitaho
Dusty Streets And Donkeys Seashells, Sunsets And A Glassy Sea

There can't be a child in the world who ever went to the seaside village of Peitaho on the Bay of Chihli and didn't look back on it with wonder that such a place ever existed at all. But it did. Latitude 39.50 degrees N and longitude 119.30 degrees E I found once in Goode's index. It was truly an idyllic place, created for a child's summer. We spent three magical summers there when we lived in Tientsin.

As with most foreign families, Mother went with my sister Connie and me and servants, especially Amah, leaving Father at home with Shao and I suppose a substitute cook. We traveled by train to a junction a few miles short of Peitaho where we transferred to a smaller train for the rest of the trip.

On the train ride, we passed small clay villages and willow trees drifting over ponds. We saw farmers in faded blue jackets digging in the fields, wearing the pagoda-shaped hats that we would soon be wearing ourselves in Peitaho. And then there would be the clusters of small children staring wide-eyed as our train rolled by. Some were stark naked. Some simply had pants open at the back, the sensible Chinese way we always thought of making it unnecessary to pull pants down in times of need.

There was always an element of danger because of the everlasting threat of bandits along the way who had the bad habit of blowing up bridges. There was one heart-stopping masterpiece of bridgework, long and with a frightening drop to the gorge below, that seemed to appeal to bandits the most. They had, we were always told, blown it up several times. Nobody breathed easily until our train had slowly chugged its way across the bridge and an eternity later reached the opposite side. But Peitaho was worth every hair-raising moment of that train ride.

It was not much more than a rustic village when we were there, made up of three clusters of summerhouses called East Cliff, Rocky Point and West Cliff. They were connected by a dusty road of hard-packed dirt, bordered by donkey paths that threaded their way down the coastline. Smaller roads turned off from it, most of them leading to the houses that dotted the cliffs, all with wide verandas overlooking the sparkling blue sea.

There were no cars in Peitaho then, so we were met at the station not only with rickshaws but also shaggy grey donkeys with immaculate white cloths draped over their saddles.

All winter these donkeys worked for their masters in a city near Peitaho called Shanhaikwan, or mountain-sea-gate, because the city lies where the mountain reaches the sea at the very end of the Great Wall of China. Each day, the donkey's master hung on its back two baskets filled with dried salt from the sea. Up the rocky mountain path would trot the donkey. When the salt had been sold, the donkey would trot back down again, this time with heavy bundles of pine logs on its back. Only to do it all over again! For the donkeys, coming to Peitaho in the summer must have seemed as much a holiday as it was for the children riding them.

"Young missy, take my donkey!"

"Young master, best donkey here!"

While their owners pleaded with the children pouring from the train, the donkeys stood patiently dusting flies off themselves with a soft swish, swish of their tails. Who cared if the hot summer air was thick with their pungent smells? We loved those donkeys, smells and all. What would summer in Peitaho be without them?

I had a problem about the donkeys, however. I've always supposed I was the only child in Peitaho who did. Much as I loved them, I was afraid to ride one. So when we went on excursions anywhere at all, my sister and friends rode donkeys, but I either walked with Mother or rode ignominiously with her in a rickshaw, all the while envying those bold, brave donkey riders.

At any rate, even my sister did not ride a donkey when we disembarked from the train. We all walked or took rickshaws to our house. Donkey rides would come later.

The house we first had in Peitaho was, like our next one, in Rocky Point. Each summer we shared a house with another family, and this time it was with a mother and six-year-old daughter. Later we were to become very good friends, but that summer my sister, ten, and I nine, considered ourselves above a six-year- old, and such things as her going-to-bed ritual with her mother.

"Good-night!"

"Good-night!" "Sleep tight!"

"So the bed bugs won't bite!"

The same silly thing night after night. Well! The house was large with verandas that reached around three sides on two floors. But we had no view of the sea from them, because the house was set behind a dense grove of trees. We had to walk through them on a rocky path to get to the beach.

Perhaps because I was still only nine, I don't remember nearly as much about summer in that house as I do the house we were to have the following two summers. But I especially remember that upstairs veranda where we slept. Our beds were right in middle of the veranda protected by mosquito nets hung from the ceiling. Therefore there was no wall anywhere near my bed. No wall! No wall with a sliding panel where a hand could creep out or a stiff dead body to fall out. I finally, at long last, could sleep with my head up on the pillow, out from under the blanket!

The second thing I remember about the veranda was the day Bradley came racing over to our house. George, Bradley, Johnny Boy and their mother were also in Peitaho. And Bradley had news for me.

"I have something to tell you!" he whispered importantly. He had run all the way from their house and was panting with excitement.

"What?" I asked, of course.

"I can't tell you here," said Bradley. "It's private. Is there anyone on the veranda?"

"No," I said. We only used the veranda for afternoon naps or sleeping at night, and it was still morning. So up we went, and perched on my bed.

"Well," said Bradley. "Mother just had a talk with us and told us something. She said I'm not supposed to tell anyone."

I'm sure "anyone" included me. In fact, it was more than likely me, as his mother knew what good friends we were.

"If I tell you, you can't tell anyone else," said Bradley. "Promise?"

"Promise," I said easily, for who else did I have to tell anyway?

"Do you know where babies come from?" asked Bradley.

"From mothers," I said. Had Bradley come racing over to ask me a silly question like that? "Yes," said Bradley, "but do you know how babies get started."

"No," I replied. The truth was that I was nine years old and had never given a moment's thought to the subject. I had just barely learned to tell time by then, so why would I be thinking about how babies got started? They were just there and that was that.

"Don't you want to know?" asked Bradley.

As I had never thought about it, why would I want to know anything about it? I just shrugged. But Bradley was determined to impart this great new piece of knowledge to me, needed or not, so he then did. When I finally figured out exactly what he was talking about, I was shocked. It was just too dreadful. Who could have ever imagined anything like that? But of course I didn't believe him. Not for one minute. I finally decided he had made the whole thing up. Bradley liked teddy bear teas and dolls, but he was, after all, still a boy. And boys had stupid boy thoughts. His mother could never have fed him such a story. I put the whole subject out of my mind.

Perhaps I shouldn't have. Some time later, back in Tientsin I fell madly in love with Franchot Tone, a famous movie star. He wasn't in any movie I believe my mother and father would have allowed us to see, so I think I just fell in love with his picture in one of my sister's Photoplay magazines. She let me cut it out, and I slept with it under my pillow. This wasn't merely monkeying around with SOCONY bachelors. This was true, mad, passionate love!

One day, I had come up to the table in our living room where Mother and three ladies were playing mah-jongg. When they realized that I was standing there, the subject they had been discussing was quickly dropped. But I had heard enough of the gossip. I had heard the words "love baby." Someone was having a "love baby!"

So that's how it began. You fell in love and a baby got started. Never mind that nonsense I had heard via Bradley. "Love baby" meant that I was in danger of having Franchot Tone's baby. How could I possibly explain Franchot's baby to my parents? That night I did not sleep with his picture under my pillow. All I could hope was that this birth-control precaution wasn't too late.

But in Peitaho, Bradley's great revelation had indeed faded quickly from my mind. Peitaho offered way too many things to do to give any further thought to such a silly subject.

Still, it was really the following two summers I remember most. One of the reasons was because of the one-story cottage we had then, perched on a cliff, with a wide veranda overlooking the sea, a perfect Peitaho cottage!

We shared this one with another mother and two little boys. We didn't like the idea of the two boys spending so much time sitting on their potties with their Amah hovering over them in our shared living room and veranda, but their mother was a good friend of ours, and we liked her as well. So we just went around pretending the boys on their potties weren't there.

Otherwise, summers were idyllic. Sunny days almost always began with the short walk to the long flight of stone stairs leading to the beach at the foot of the cliff where we would spend our whole morning until tiffin. Our beach, like others dotting the coast was lined with grass huts, or pengs, where mothers sat. More often, though, it was amahs sitting there knitting or gossiping as they kept watchful eyes fastened on their precious charges swimming or wading in the sea.

The water was often smooth as a lily pond and clear as blue crystal. We could look down and see right to the velvety sand ripples beneath our feet. There was no big thundering surf, just tiny gentle waves lapping the shore, but there were two manned junks that were stopping points before the raft was reached. My brave heroine sister, of course, always swam to the raft while I hovered around the first junk. Once, with my sister beside me, I actually braved it all the way past the second junk to the raft. But then I had to sit there worrying about getting back, so I didn't try it again.

We swam, we floated, we paddled and splashed. When the season was right, we collected slippery jellyfish tentacles and laid them out on the sand or the floor of a junk. We dug holes in the sand. We, of course, made sand castles. We collected shells, mostly tellinas lined with lavender and rose. They were like little paint palettes of the sea that echoed the colors of the breathtaking lavender and rose sunsets we watched from our veranda. And all the while we baked in the sun. By the end of the summer, our faces, our shoulders, our arms and legs were nut brown.

We never used any sunscreen. Nobody knew about the dangers of the sun on the skin then. Mother might have warned us about wearing hats, as sunstroke was a worry. But on our first day, we couldn't be dragged away from the beach. And though one would think experience would have taught us something, it never seemed to. We would spend the very first morning, and sometimes even the whole in misery with Mother daubing our flaming painful shoulders with tea and vinegar. Then came the blisters and the peeling. This happened on a regular basis every summer. We never learned, but more likely probably didn't care. We just accepted it as a fact of summer.

When we returned from the beach, we would have a wash in non-salt water. This took place in a shower or tub. A very few houses had self-contained water storage tanks and their own electric generators, but most houses did not. Our house had a courtyard behind it. At the back of the courtyard were the servants' quarters. On one side was a grass peng with a SOCONY gasoline can perched on top that Coolie kept filled with water. The can had a shower spout below it.

The tub was a tin tub set up in our bedroom. Coolie also brought warm water in for that, but it was difficult carting in pots of water from a stove way in the back of the court, so we had to wash in a few inches of lukewarm water in the tub.

We followed the same routine we had in Hankow, where my sister always went into the tub first, leaving me to climb in with a cold, soaking wet towel, and sit on the plug. So in the Peitaho shower I was often left with water dribbling to a sudden stop. As for the tub, I had to rinse off in almost cold water well salted from my sister's swim in the sea, while sitting on a liberal sprinkling of sand at the bottom. I really do wonder why I never complained, but I never did. Looking back, I believe the only chance I ever had was in the sea itself. There, there was enough water for all, no plugs, and I even had my own dry bathing suit!

Because there was no running water, there was of course no flushing toilet. What we had was the equivalent of an outhouse in the courtyard. Except for a few lucky people, almost everyone had them. They were serviced by men with horse-drawn carts that were called "honey carts." Somebody with a rare sense of humor must have named these. Never has a more inappropriate name be given anything in this world. One tried never, never to be caught walking behind a "honey cart" on a hot summer day!

But uncomfortable bathing arrangements, and no flushing toilets were a small price to pay for our wonderful Peitaho summers. In a way, they probably even added to the enchantment.

We sometime returned to the beach after tiffin, but more often we just lolled around the house. In the afternoons, almost everyone took naps. It was difficult not to want to. Peitaho seemed to grow very still, with only the drowsy hum of cicadas, which we called by the much more picturesque name of "scissor grinders," or the braying of a rebellious donkey to break the silence. I would go to bed with a Tiger Tim Annual, carefully open the red and gold wrapper of a Nestle's chocolate bar, peel down the thin silver foil, and slowly nibble just three squares on them to keep them going as long as possible. Why three? It wasn't that I wasn't allowed more. It's just what I did. Peitaho was a place to follow wonderful familiar patterns, and that was mine.

After naptime, we often bivouacked on the porch in one of the large wicker chairs with their flowered cretonne pillows, and went on reading. Mother read, too, or sat and sewed or knitted. Sometimes she had a bridge game going, or more often mah-jongg. The click-click-click of mah-jongg tiles became for us yet another familiar Peitaho sound.

Frequent visitors to our verandas in the afternoon were traveling Chinese salesmen. They brought with them a whole department store full of treasures in faded blue cloth bundles hung one on each end of a bamboo pole carried on their shoulders. They would lay the bundles on the floor of the veranda, peel them open, and lay out an incredible display for us. Beautiful cloisonné bowls of multi-colored flowers set in black. Porcelain vases, with scrolled designs set in yellow, pale green, or blue. Snuff bottles of turquoise and rose quartz. Carved ivory elephants. Jade brooches and earrings. Hand-embroidered table linens. This traveling salesman would keep pulling things out of his bundles until half our veranda floor was covered. It really was a whole store full!

In the evenings we sat on the veranda to watch the breathtaking sunsets. Sometimes there would be rainstorms with frightening cracks of thunder that seemed to shake the house. But, as if by way of an apology, these would always be followed by even more spectacular sunsets.

Then it was nightfall, and as there was no electricity, our oil lanterns were lit. We read by oil lantern, and Mother and her friends played mah-jongg by oil lantern. When we turned down our bedroom lanterns to go to sleep at last, it was often to the comforting, familiar click-click of mahjongg tiles.

And then the next day, it would start all over again.

But once in a while our beach-going would be interrupted by a trip to visit friends in East Cliff. Or a trip to the Lotus Hills. As we didn't wear shorts in those days, my sister and I put on our cotton dresses instead of climbing into our bathing suits.

"And you must wear your hats!" said Mother.

"Yes, we know," we said. We didn't need to be reminded. We never knew anyone who had actually had it, but who was there who would risk having the dreaded sunstroke? Our hats were not the western style with brims. These were the same pagoda-shaped kind we had seen the farmers wearing. Everyone wore them in Peitaho. A string of children on donkeys looked like a parade of traveling mushrooms, bobbing along in those hats.

Whenever we were going on an excursion, word got out very quickly, probably by the servant grapevine. There would be a cluster of donkeys at our garden gate, each driver pointing out the great qualities of his donkey. Unfortunately, only one member of our family would choose one, my sister. Mother would walk, or take a rickshaw. With, alas, me.

En route to the Lotus Hills, we often passed one of the men who fashioned intricate figures of rice paste around a stick. Right before our eyes, we watched his nimble fingers turn out small brightly colored masterpieces, a squatting fisherman complete with lantern, straw cape, and fishing pole, a fierce tiger, a white dog, a green dragon, or a Chinese actress with a narrow, white-powdered face, almond eyes, and a costume of peony pink and pomegranate red. Mother let us stop to watch, but not to buy one until our return trip.

Once we went with George, Bradley, their mother and Johnny Boy, who was too young to ride a donkey. He rode with his mother in a rickshaw. This was embarrassing, but not embarrassing enough, I guess, to get me on a donkey.

When we arrived at the Lotus Hills, the mothers plus Johnny Boy went to sit on the broad pavilion of the Lotus Hills teahouse, to meet with other friends and have tea. George, Bradley, my sister and I with a couple of other friends we hooked up with, generally ran around, but especially played hide and seek.

"Olly, olly oxen, all in free!" we sang out from the stone monument atop a large grey stone turtle whose back we climbed and sat on.

After a while we all decided to visit our mothers on the pavilion. It was then that Johnny Boy whispered something in his mother's ear. The next minute she was rushing him across the pavilion filled with other tea- drinking ladies, and some children as well.

"I don't want to go big umpies! I want to go wee-wee!" shouted Johnny Boy at the top of his lungs.

Well, at least my worst crime was not riding a donkey. What, for example, if Johnny Boy had been my little brother!

CHAPTER X

Peitaho
Still Of Mice And Sadness And A Scary Journey

One night in Peitaho, my sister and I heard some tiny scrabbling, scratching sounds coming from a drawer in our dresser.

"Are you awake?" asked my sister.

"Yes, are you?" I replied, not very brilliantly.

"Do you hear that?" she asked.

"Yes," I replied. I didn't need to ask what she meant.

"Well, I'm going to see what it is," said my sister, and promptly lit the little oil lamp sitting on the table between our beds.

I jumped out of bed along with her, and in our bare feet, we tiptoed over to the dresser. She gently opened the drawer and shone the lantern in it. There was a nest made of paper that had been used to line the drawer. In it were six tiny, wriggling pink baby mice, their eyes still closed. The mother mouse had scurried away as soon as the drawer started to open. Was she watching from somewhere, terrified?

"What are we going to do?" I asked.

"Nothing now," said my sister, carefully closing the drawer.

"I suppose we'll have to tell Mother," I said. "I suppose we will," said my sister.

And, stupidly, that's exactly what we did the next morning. Coolie was, of course, immediately dispatched to our room, and we were told that the mice had been drowned.

Drowned! Somehow it had never occurred to us that something so terrible would happen to those tiny pink babies. Well, did we think they would be put up for adoption and homes found for them? The truth was we didn't think at all, although probably would have suggested something like that when questioned. But drowned! And dumped out on the garbage heap behind our house.

There wasn't much we could do about it that day. But there was that night. Oil lamps off, we lay in bed, keeping ourselves awake and waiting. When we no longer heard the soft murmurs of voices from the two mothers in our house, or from the servants' quarters at the back of the courtyard, we crept out of bed.

It was warm out, so we didn't need to put anything over our

cotton pajamas. We didn't bother to put on socks, but with eyes growing used to the darkness we managed to tie on our Keds over bare feet. Then, with me clutching a bath towel, and my sister her flashlight, we crept out through the courtyard, and out the back gate to the garbage heap. The baby mice were there, and four of them twitched their tiny pink tails when we touched them. We picked them up, wrapped them in the towel, and took them back to our room.

Their nest was gone, so we pulled paper out from under the clothes in another drawer, and tore it up to make another nice, cozy little nest. Then we put the babies into it. Of course, nobody bothered to check that drawer. And it seemed that nobody checked the garbage heap either. Why would they? A dead mouse is a dead mouse, and certainly nobody planned to have funeral services for them.

My sister and I made it a point not to open the drawer again, not even when we heard more scratching, scrabbling sounds coming from it. We did not open it again until there were no more sounds. When we finally opened it, very, very carefully, the mice were gone. We gathered up the nest, and neither of us ever mentioned this to anyone. Not ever!

This is a Peitaho story with two-thirds of a happy ending . . . four out of six baby mice saved. Another story did not have any happy ending, and it didn't seem that it should have happened during a happy holiday in Peitaho.

It was really an ordinary Peitaho summer day, going to the beach, napping, sitting on the veranda watching the sunset. But Mother had told us just before dinner that Amah had received a letter earlier that day telling her that her married daughter had died of cholera.

Cholera! We had had no reason to think about cholera in Peitaho. Was there an epidemic in Tientsin where she had died? Nobody had mentioned it. Amah hadn't even said anything about her daughter that day. She didn't ask Mother for the day off. She behaved just as she always did, quietly padding about, picking up our wet bathing suits, sweeping up sand we had brought in on our feet from the beach. So we put it right out of our minds.

That night we played card games of Fish on the veranda. When we were ready for bed, we found the covers turned down just as they always were. We read by the light of our oil lamp just as we always did, then turned it off, and fell peacefully asleep.

But sometime in the middle of the night, we were awakened by frightening sounds that filled the dark night, filled the silent courtyard, and finally, filled our room. They were like sounds I had never heard before, the sounds of someone moaning, and sobbing and wailing. I pulled the covers over my head, but it was impossible to drown them out. I knew what it was. It was our Amah finally pouring out her grief for her lost child. I lay awake for a long time overcome with pity and terror.

The next morning, my sister was owl eyed as I was. She must have been lying awake as I did. But we never said anything to each other about it. Nor did I know what to say to Amah. I was just as tongue tied as when I was five years old. But Amah came next day to make our beds and pick up our wet bathing suits and sweep up the sand we had brought in from the beach. She was our Amah again.

But Cholera had once been just a word. It never would be again.

This took place during a summer vacation that almost never happened. It was our last summer in Tientsin before we were to on home leave. When we returned it would be to Shanghai, and from there would probably no longer be spending summers in Peitaho.

"I don't think you girls and Mother will be able to go to Peitaho this summer," Father told us one morning.

"But why not?" we wailed. "Bandits," said Father.

Well, we all knew about bandits. From as early as we could remember Father had told us about near-encounters with bandits when he had traveled into the country to sell lamp oil and candles in Chinese villages. Bandits were an old story to us. And hadn't we had to worry about them every summer anyway when we crossed that scary bridge? Why would they keep us from Peitaho on this our last summer in Tientsin?

"Because" we were told, "bandits are causing a great deal of trouble this year. It's too dangerous."

But just when we had resigned ourselves to a long, hot summer in Tientsin, it appeared that the U.S. vice consul had decided to take his family and serve as "protection" to other families who wanted to go to Peitaho. So we were told that we would be going after all along with our same friend with her two little boys. My sister and I lost no time racing to our room to pack bathing suits, games, and books. Pots, pans, clothing, food and other such non- essentials we could leave to Mother to worry about.

It was doubly frightening crossing that high bridge, but as the bandits had conveniently not blown it up as they often did, we made it across and arrived safely at four in the afternoon at the junction where we would meet the local train taking us the rest of the way to Peitaho. We waved off the train that had brought us, and then waited. And waited. And waited. It was six o'clock, two hours later, and the local train still had not arrived.

And then against the strong advice of the U.S. vice consul, Mother decided to negotiate with a driver with a flat, mule-drawn cart to take the three of us, plus the friend and her two small boys, and go off on our own through the fields to Peitaho. The mule owner assured Mother he could get us to Peitaho in half an hour. The end result of this was that at about six thirty, two lone American women with two young girls, my sister and me, and two small boys set off on a flat cart pulled by a skinny mule driven by its Chinese owner, who could have, for all we knew, been a bandit himself.

Before anyone quite realized what was happening, the driver led his mule right through the middle of a pond, as careless as if we'd been so many sacks of potatoes. Filthy pond water splashed all over us. My sister and I clutched one another. The little boys started screaming. Then, soaked and shivering in the night air, we went bumping and thumping along over deep-rutted mud paths through miles and miles of dense, head-high gau-liang, a type of Chinese grain, and a wonderful hiding place for bandits.

We were still traveling on the cart when the sun set entirely. We were in the middle of primitive nowhere, with no streetlights, and no policemen or telephones if we got into trouble. And of course, we were in trouble. We were then in total darkness with only a tiny lantern swinging on the front of the cart hanging precariously under the mule's tail. I believe Mother knew before the driver even told us, that we were lost.

It turned out that the local train came right after we left. It arrived in Peitaho less than half an hour later. It was four hours before we arrived in Peitaho. If there is such a thing as a guardian angel, one must surely have been watching over us.

It was two years before we were to return to Peitaho. The only ones to go were my sister and I, leaving behind our mother and father. I was fourteen and my sister fifteen. We had already had one adventure going to Peitaho.

Unknown to us, however, we were yet to have another one. And this one was to be the China adventure of our lives.

CHAPTER XI

Shanghai
Sas, And Peitaho Redux

Shanghai!

Shanghai was where Mother, as a young girl of sixteen had come from Russia, at seventeen had entered the Harvard Medical School of China as a nurse probationer, and graduated as a full-fledged nurse. Shanghai was where Father, who had left his acting career with the Flying A film company in California and been selling oil for the lamps of China in Tsining, had come bringing with him the head of the rabid dog that had bitten him. And finally, Shanghai where Mother and Father had met, escaped the enormous wedding planned for them, and eloped in a sampan, a perfect Hollywood film ending, courtesy of the Flying A and the Harvard Medical School of China!

Shanghai! Where I did nothing more thrilling than go to school. So, glamorous though its reputation, Shanghai meant only one thing to me. A new school I had to get used to.

When we arrived in Shanghai, we stayed first at a pension in the French concession, moved into a small apartment on the fifth floor of the Picardy Apartments on Rue Petain, and I, twelve going on thirteen, walked three blocks to enter the seventh grade of the fabled Shanghai American School. Well, I didn't know it was so fabled then, which was probably just as well. I was just as nervous as I always was starting a new school. And yes indeed, I had lost what little breakfast I could get down, and probably would do so for at least two more days.

So focused on my health problems, blood drinking and all the rest, no one ever bothered to tell me that I was actually bright. I think I found it out for the first time at the Shanghai American School when I insisted on coloring my geography map book all over again because I had erased a hole in one of the pages. Everyone thought this silly, until seventh-grade teacher, Mrs. Huestis, announced that I was a "credit to the class." This is not something to endear a person to their classmates. However, nobody held this against me, though from then I was nicknamed Brainwave. Brainwave! What a great nickname. That was depressing, but I was actually popular. And for the first time I now had girl friends of my own. I didn't have to trail around after my sister sharing hers. And, of course, "boys" were beginning to enter the picture. In a way.

I had three special friends, Josephine, Geraldine, and Lella, but the one with whom I shared "secrets" was Geraldine. I was in love again, and so was Geraldine, she with a boy a class above us, and me with a high school junior. We dreamt about these boys, and then couldn't wait to tell each other about the dream we had just had.

Geraldine actually knew her "love" slightly. Very slightly, it was true. But mine was love from afar. I knew it was hopeless. My existence was unknown to him. I think he held a door open for me once, and that was as close as I ever got to him in person. I couldn't wait to tell Geraldine about it. But I had her photograph me holding open The Columbian, our school annual, to a page that had his picture on it. Good grief!

Boys in my class, the real thing, didn't interest me much at all. We started having dances with boys, but girls danced with each other as well. I was devoted to Geraldine. Once when we were dancing together, three different boys came and tapped her on the shoulder, cutting in to dance with me. I had no intention of leaving Geraldine alone in the middle of the dance floor, so ignored the boys. Each one returned to the "stag" line with an embarrassed shrug. I had no idea that this was not only impolite, but truly idiotic behavior.

I had already shot up to five foot seven inches in the seventh grade, and was skinny and still totally hopeless in sports. So brainy and popular though I might have been in school, I was always one of the last ones chosen for team sports. I couldn't blame anybody. If you were out to win, you wouldn't want anyone like me on the team. It wasn't until I was a junior in high school in America, that all at once I became a basketball "star." Five foot seven inches and skinny did have its advantages then!

But so it was. That was school. It was in Shanghai, China, but it was an American school, and could have been in Timbuktu for all the difference it made. Outside of school, I still had to have Amah trailing along with me when I went to visit Geraldine. That was it.

There is one thing, though, I especially remember about the time when we were in Shanghai, and it had nothing to do with school, or girl friends, or even boys. It was something that happened the first summer we were in Shanghai.

Louise, whose father was head of the SOCONY office as he had been in Hankow, was briefly in Shanghai when we were there. She invited me to spend one night with their family on the SOCONY launch, anchored in the Whangpu River. I remember waking up in the middle of the night and looking out the window. A full moon shone down on the river, but there was no river traffic at that time of night. Then all at once a magnificent junk appeared, cutting majestically through the water in total silence. Silent, magnificent, magic . . . I kept my eyes fastened on it until it disappeared. It was like a dream, a wish. It was China.

That summer, however, except for my night on the river, was remarkably humdrum. We didn't go to Peitaho or Kuling. We just stayed and sweltered in our apartment with nothing much to do. Mother and Dad had decided not to join the Columbia Country Club, but instead joined the French Club. Neither my sister nor I liked swimming in their pool as we never had any friends there. Once in a while we went to the Columbia Country Club as guests of George and Bradley. That we did enjoy, and whereas we always had ginger snaps after swimming in the Tientsin Country Club pool, in Shanghai it was always Eskimo pies. Real, genuine American Eskimo pies "Made in Shanghai!"

Then came the summer of 1937.

"How would you like to go to Peitaho?" my sister asked me.

My sister liked to tease me. Or was it teasing?

I couldn't help remembering the time early one morning in Tientsin, the day after Christmas, when she woke me before daybreak to ask what I thought was in our Christmas stockings. Mother always managed to have something sticking up at the top of the stockings hung at the foot of our beds. This was probably the most exciting thing about our Christmases, lying there, guessing the mysterious object before the great moment of actually finding out. Or perhaps my sister wasn't teasing, but only miserable as I was that it was all over for another year.

Was that what this question was all about? I was older now, and that kind of teasing didn't work quite so well on me any more.

"Don't be silly," I said. "Mother won't leave Daddy alone in Shanghai, and that's that." Well, I knew Mother had been willing to leave good-looking Father on his own in Tientsin, but she wasn't willing to leave him alone in Shanghai. Whether true or not, wasn't there all sorts of wickedness and vice, of which I knew nothing about but vividly imagined, supposedly rampant in Shanghai? Wickedness and vice! I didn't blame Mother at all.

"I didn't mean with Mother," said my sister.

"Dr. Thompson, my Latin teacher, owns a house in Peitaho. I found out she takes summer boarders from SAS. I asked if she'd take us, and she said she would. What's the matter? Don't you want to go? You're not afraid, are you?"

Afraid? Of course I was afraid. We'd never been away from our Mother in our lives. I certainly did not want to go. This was not a birthday party I didn't want. This was not a scary movie I wished I hadn't gone to. It wasn't just going to visit my friend Geraldine with Amah trailing along, to discuss the latest dream du jour. This would be honest-to- goodness leaving Mother for a whole summer! The thought was terrifying.

"No, I'm not afraid!" I hurled back.

"Good!" said my sister. "Then all we have to do is persuade Mother and Daddy to let us go."

Saved! I was relieved at once. It was quite certain that the answer would be "No! Absolutely not!"

I was wrong. It took some doing on my sister's part, but as I was just as unhappy about saying "no" as I was saying "yes," and she was determined, Mother and Father were finally persuaded that we could go.

Arrangements were made, and almost before I could blink, I found myself miserably on the train with my sister and Dr. Thompson, waving to Mother, bravely smiling, and Father through the train window en route to Peitaho.

Moments later, a truly amazing thing happened. As soon as they had disappeared from sight, all my fears and anxieties floated away. Vanished. Gone. All I could think was that we were going to Peitaho! Furthermore, I hadn't disgraced myself by being a big baby about it. And after all, wasn't I under the protection of my heroine sister? What had I been so worried about? I curled up on the train bench and happily watched Shanghai disappear.

CHAPTER XII

Peitaho Farewell
Of "Incidents", Us Two, And The U.S. Navy

What I've since wondered is if Mother and Father knew that trouble was brewing that summer in China. On the other hand, wasn't trouble always brewing somewhere in China? We used to get "worry" letters from Grandma in California, and clippings from the LA TIMES advising us of all the fearful things happening in China, most of which we knew nothing about.

If there were any rumblings of "trouble brewing" they must not have been loud enough for our parents to hear them, or we would certainly never have been on that train going to Peitaho with Dr. Thompson.

Peitaho was the same wonderful place it always had been. My sister and I shared a lovely big room right beside the spacious veranda of Dr. Thompson's cottage. Sunlight splashed through tall

Victorian windows onto the faded roses of old wallpaper. We had to share a double-bed of scrolled white iron; this was the first time we'd ever had to share a bed, and for some reason, we didn't mind that at all. We also shared a painted white dresser, but had two wicker chairs, all resting on cool, bare waxed pine floors. Except for the double bed, it was very much like the room we had shared in another Peitaho house.

"Aren't you glad we came?" my sister said, when we saw our room.

Well, I'd been glad the moment our train glided out of the station in Shanghai. I'd been glad when we stepped off the train steps into the hot, dusty station asleep in the Peitaho sun. I'd been glad when we saw the grey donkeys and heard the scissor grinders singing their summer songs in the mimosa trees. Glad! Glad! Glad! I suppose I should have felt guilty that homesickness could vanish so quickly. But I didn't.

The familiar Peitaho routine began at once of the same sunny days at the beach, the same shabby grey donkeys (which I was still afraid to ride, but loved nonetheless), and the same sleepy afternoons. The same list of every familiar thing! But this time we had added arriving with comforting regularity lots of letters from home, plus boxes filled with hams, fruit, cookies, and naturally, Nestle's chocolate bars. Mother was determined that we were not going to starve to death!

And, of course, there was lots of reading on the veranda. That summer, feeling very grown up and proud of myself at fourteen, I ploughed through Anthony Adverse and Gone With the Wind.

Only one mildly unhappy event happened to me that whole summer. I felt grown up enough as well to bargain with one of the traveling Chinese salesmen who came to Dr. Thompson's veranda one afternoon. When he unpacked his faded blue cloth bundles, I spotted something I wanted desperately. It was another tiny thing to keep in a drawer in my rosewood chest. I still remember it, a one and one half inch little covered pot carved of turquoise, my birthstone. I was already the proud owner of a gold ring with a tiny turquoise stone set in it that my father had given me.

However, being that child of old China, I knew I must not pay the asking price for the little pot. One never paid the first asking price for anything. I must bargain for it and bring the price down. I knew of friends who had sat all afternoon drinking cups of tea to negotiate a proper price for something they had to have. So I made an offer. The salesman looked offended and made a counter offer. I inched up on mine. But in the end, I apparently had insulted him enough that he packed the turquoise pot back into his bundle. So much for my bargaining skills! And I really, really had wanted it that little turquoise treasure. I have wanted it forever.

I suppose I could consider that I had learned a lesson, though I'm not sure what it was, unless to accept that I wasn't as grown up or as it, the lesson I learned in bargaining wouldn't have done me much good thereafter. In America, you pay the price printed on the ticket. Period. Well, unless you are buying a house or a car or a company, which, of course, is quite another story.

And so the summer went. That is until "trouble brewing" became much more than that. Newspapers were mailed to Peitaho from Shanghai, and Dr. Thompson read to us one July morning at breakfast.

"Well, Japan has invaded China!"

She went on to read about the Marco Polo incident in Peking. Long afterwards, we knew that was the foretelling of World War II. But this was never called a "war." It was always referred to as just an "incident." Then Dr. Thompson read to us that Japanese forces had occupied Tientsin on July 30. Still just an "incident."

But this "incident" was only a faint distant echo in peaceful, sunny Peitaho. And if anyone was worried, those worries were soon put to rest. After all, the USS TULSA, an American destroyer had been dispatched at once to stand guard off the coast of Peitaho. On August 9, the Tulsa left, but the USS JOHN D. FORD steamed in to replace it. Fighting ships flying the flag of the United States in full sight of everyone! Why would anyone worry with them in Shanghai? At once, though, arrangements were made for us to leave Peitaho. We would go as we had come, by train.

And then, Dr. Thompson read again from the newspaper.

"Well, they've blown up the bridge!" Blown up the bridge! Who blew it up?

"Was it the Japanese?" my sister asked. "Or was it bandits?"

I thought it more likely to have been bandits.

This wasn't surprising. Hadn't we heard about those bandits for as long as I could remember? Wicked bandits with the long mustaches, squinting black eyes, and evil smiles, or so I had pictured them. I believed they were at the bottom of everything.

"Probably the farmers themselves," said Dr. Thompson calmly, "to keep the tracks from being used by their enemies. But there certainly will be no more trains coming in or out of Peitaho bringing newspapers, or mail, or passengers."

Passengers! That meant us, didn't it? So how were we going to get to Shanghai?

"By ship, of course," Dr. Thompson reassured us.

By then, the only means of communication with the outside world was via amateur wireless sets or the United States vessel stationed in the channel. On August 12, the first message we received came in via amateur wireless, addressed to my sister.

"We have been requested by our Shanghai Agency to confirm with you direct," read the message from the Kailan Mining

Administration, which operated the ships, "that accommodation has been reserved for yourself and sister by the SS CHANGON to Shanghai sailing on or about the 5th of September."

But five days later, another message arrived. "Owing to the present situation, we are instructed to accept no passengers by the Administration's vessels for Shanghai until further notice."

Then between August 12 and August 17, "Bloody Saturday" happened, the days the bombs fell in the heart of Shanghai, on a street teeming with pushing, shoving, frightened refugees who had fled the countryside for the safety of the city.

That day, our mother had been persuaded by Dolly Loo, her close Chinese friend, to accompany her to a bank on the Shanghai Bund, and from there to take her ailing son to a doctor. They were on the Bund during the terrible moments when the bombs fell. The impact lifted the car right off the street, Mother told us.

A radio message dated August 17, intercepted from a Shanghai radio station, was delivered to us telling us that we were to stay on with Dr. Thompson for the present, but that our parents might go to Manila in the Philippines.

Mother said later that there was a worse moment for her than being caught on the Bund when the bombs fell. It was when she stood with Father on the jetty waiting for the launch that was to take them to the SS PRESIDENT HOOVER, the ocean liner that would take hundreds of evacuees to Manila. She had to leave behind her two girls, now stranded on the north coast of China, praying that somehow the United States Navy could somehow make good its assurance of bringing them all together again.

We received a message that came via the USS JOHN D. FORD telling us that our parents were now both in Manila. We were now separated from them now only the miles between Shanghai and Peitaho, but by an ocean, and a war.

I suppose that we, particularly me, who as has been made clear, was easily frightened by just about everything, including big dogs, Chinese funeral horns, riding donkeys, and of course, entering the third grade, should have been terrified by the thought of being stranded in Peitaho away from our parents. But we were not. Neither of us. Which included me.

Why would we be frightened? Peitaho lay peaceful and quiet in the summer sun. Scissor grinders sang their songs. Donkeys brayed.

We still went down to the beach to swim in the glassy sea, and gather seashells. And then there was that destroyer in plain sight out there. We knew we were under the protection of the American flag. We were perfectly safe. Nobody else seemed worried, so why should we? Why should I?

And there was something else. I was in love again, this time busy falling in love with the whole U.S. Navy. Wives of American businessmen, stranded in Peitaho as we all were, decided they might as well enjoy themselves, so gave dinner parties for the officers aboard the destroyer. Now being "young ladies" of fourteen and fifteen, we had been invited to the dinners. This was thrilling enough, but at one, a young ensign was nice enough to sit next to me and actually hold a conversation with heart-palpitating me. I could hardly breathe. Quite naturally, I fell in love with him at once. Along with the rest of the U.S. Navy, of course!

Mother's first love when she was a student nurse in Shanghai had been a US naval officer, a surgeon. It was World War I that kept them apart or they might have married. Mother learned later that Dr. Vickery never married. But she always loved the Navy, and has always remembered her Navy officer. I guess I wasn't my mother's daughter for nothing!

However, when the seriousness of the situation now became more evident, Peitaho began to dig in for a possible long siege. My sister and I were two young girls separated from our parents and alone in Peitaho. Americans took us into their protective arms at once. When a school was organized by the American community in a church in East Cliff, it was determined that Rocky Point was too far for us to commute to the school. An American family volunteered quickly to take us in.

On September 3, the USS ALDEN, steamed in to replace the USS FORD as guardian of the channel. Then, sometime between the hours of midnight and four on the morning of September 25, a second destroyer slipped into the channel to anchor beside the ALDEN. It was the USS PEARY, sent there to rescue Americans who wished to leave Peitaho.

As it turned out, very few people had that wish. This wasn't surprising. Wives vacationing with children didn't want to leave husbands behind in China. And nobody thought anything could happen to them. How could it when they had the US Navy guarding them? Furthermore, just as in the past, any trouble flaring up in China would most certainly flare right back down again. They would stay put in Peitaho.

But my sister and I had received word that we were to leave Peitaho on that destroyer. Just as Mother and Father had been promised, the U.S. Navy was seeing to it that we would all be together again!

Our smart hostess had had a Chinese tailor quickly make wool slacks for us. She felt that climbing gangplanks and who knows what else, we should not be encumbered with skirts. It seems curious that in a country, where like many others, Chinese women wore pants, we never had. Pants are such intelligent garments. Our amahs had all worn them. But these were the first pants we had ever had. We were so grateful later that someone had had the foresight to see that it's what we were wearing.

We had been told that the PEARY would pick us up at Rocky

Point rather than East Cliff. Dawn was barely beginning to light up the sky when my sister and I climbed out of bed and into our slacks. We managed to get down some breakfast, and then rickshaws were hired to take us to the same beach where we had always gone swimming.

Now we stood there, shivering in the early morning cold fall air, waiting for the launch that was to take us to the destroyer. There were only four souls besides us who had chosen to leave Peitaho that morning, one of them an infant with her two parents. There was also another woman. She was Mrs. Lambert, who wanted to join her husband in the Philippines. She would be our guardian angel for that very remarkable journey we were about to take.

I really think that by then I should have started feeling frightened. It might have made my story more dramatic. But I wasn't frightened at all. Not even close to feeling frightened, though it almost seems dimwitted not to have been. It wasn't bravery. I had never done anything brave in my life. I suppose it was simply that we had always been protected, and I was certain nothing could possibly happen to us.

But it went beyond that. It was that we were wrapped in the flag of the United States of America. The American flag! Nobody would dare harm us. Nobody! And after all, I was only fourteen, and these were men of the United States Navy rescuing us. Fourteen-year- old me! This was exciting as it could get.

CHAPTER XIII

Between China And Philippines Cruising On The USS Chaumont

I wasn't even worried when we were standing on the Peitaho shore, and saw the USS PEARY steaming away. Without us on it! Somebody had apparently given out the wrong information. We were actually to board her right at East Cliff. So back into rickshaws we all climbed. And finally into the launch that took us to the PEARY.

As the USS PEARY pulled away from the USS ALDEN, I stood in morning mist at the top of the stairs leading down to the quarters the officers had kindly vacated for us evacuees. A light breeze blew my long hair back from my face. I felt unbelievably dramatic, standing there (in my smashing wool slacks!) gazing out across the water. I could have been in a movie scene. And then I saw someone waving from the ALDEN. Oh! Oh! Oh! Was that my ensign waving to me?

Two sailors were standing on the deck nearby, and I heard one of them say, "She isn't going to last long!"

But the fact is that "she" didn't. Never mind that terrible insult. Moments later, I barely made it to the "head" to part company with whatever breakfast I had managed to get down earlier. Then I somehow managed to climb into a top bunk in the officers' quarters, and lay there curled up and miserable for the whole day it took the ALDEN to get to Chefoo. The only consolation I had, such as it was, was that my sister of the ironclad stomach was curled up on the bunk below me, as sick as I was.

I decided that they don't call destroyers "tin cans" for nothing. Or perhaps "empty tin cans" would be more like it the way they pitch and roll, especially on a rough sea. It was probably a good thing we didn't know that because of the rough seas, the PEARY had been extensively damaged when it was tied up to the ALDEN, and we were essentially limping all the way to Chefoo, where the old World War I troop transport, the USS CHAUMONT, was already there, waiting for us.

Well, not exactly waiting for us. Actually, it was primarily making that voyage to transport the wives and children of US Navy personnel. It seemed that we were rather an extra tacked on to the passenger list way at the end. The very, very end, as it turned up. We had the feeling nobody quite knew what to do with us. We were so fortunate that we had Mrs. Lambert taking us under wing.

Having seen both of us so miserably seasick on the USS PEARY, she told us sternly that we were not to be sick on the USS CHAUMONT. She wouldn't allow it. For some reason, this was comforting, although the warning probably wasn't necessary. Even though I was quite an expert at losing my meals when starting with the third grade, and the fourth grade, and on up, I had never been sick on an ocean liner when we crossed the Pacific Ocean, nor had my sister. A destroyer was quite another thing, and the USS CHAUMONT, though a far cry from the luxury of a Robert Dollar liner, was definitely not a destroyer bobbing about on the high seas.

Even Mrs. Lambert, though, couldn't do much to lift our spirits when we were shown our "cabin." It appeared that as civilians on a ship primarily intended to evacuate families of navy personnel, we were not only at the bottom of the list, but the bottom of the ship as well. The very bottom! We climbed down a steep flight of steps, only to climb down yet another one. The room where we ended up held hundreds of bunks piled up three deep. This was a troop transport, after all. There were no portholes as we were entirely under water. The only light came from small blue lights that were on day and night. They had to be, or the room would have been in pitch dark.

When we arrived, there was only one woman and her small son in the hold. She was Russian, she told us, married to a Philippine American sailor. She looked forlorn and lonely, which didn't raise our spirits very much. We had been told that the rest of the bunks would be occupied when we came to our next port, Tsingtao. That dampened our spirits even further. All those hundreds of bunks at the bottom of the ship filled with women and probably even crying babies. This was hardly the kind of travel we were used to.

Before we were introduced to our "cabin," we were introduced to the bathrooms. The washbasin was one long cast iron sink that stretched from wall to wall. Before we had even set sail, with so many women and children now aboard occupying all the holds but our own at the bottom of the ship, the sink was already stopped up. It had rapidly filled with water, which went sloshing back and forth and over the edge of the sink as soon as we set sail.

The toilets were in another room. They consisted of a long wood bench with holes cut in it. They had no walls in front of them. They had no walls separating them. They were just bare-bone holes out there in front of anyone who might be in the room. My sister and I somehow managed incredibly to be in there when no one else was. But just in case someone should appear, she stood guard in front of me while I used one of the holes. Then I guarded her doing the same. Compared to this, our outhouse in Peitaho was the height of luxury.

Our shipmates, with whom we shared bathrooms, sleeping quarters, and the dining room, were the families of pre-World-War-II sailors, whose backgrounds were far different from what we were used to. The "salty" language my sister and I heard probably would have made our parents' hair stand on end. These were the parents, it must be remembered, who kept their girls from learning the Chinese language lest they pick up some "naughty" words!

As it turned out, we only spent one night sleeping, or at least trying to sleep, below sea level at the bottom of the ship. Mrs. Lambert was talking to the deck steward and just happened to mention that her brother was a lieutenant commander in the navy. This meant she was related to a naval officer. It followed that she was therefore entitled to a cabin. And as she had no intention of deserting us, we were included in the transaction.

The only problem was that there were no cabins available. One was unoccupied, but would be by an officer's wife and her two girls as soon as we reached Hong Kong. The deck steward, however, told us we could have the cabin until that time. Then, he said, we would be in tropical waters and it would be warm enough to sleep on deck. Moving up away from those blue lights, no portholes, and into daylight! None of us would have cared if we'd had to sleep right on the deck.

It was a tiny, basic, no-frills cabin. Even though it was intended for naval officers, the USS CHAUMONT was still a troop ship and not a luxury ocean liner. But all three of us agreed that we had never appreciated any cabin in any ship as much as this one.

We could also now even eat in the officer's mess, said the deck steward.

"I think we'll stay where we are in the enlisted dining hall," Mrs. Lambert told him. Then to us, "If that's all right with you girls."

Fine with us. Even in the short time we had been assigned to the dark hold, we had already hooked up with several of the children. The two of us, perhaps because we had moved as much as we had, easily adapted to whatever situations came our way. So for all of our protected, careful, naughty-word-free existence, we got along just fine with those pre-World- War-II rough-talking sailors' kids. And they got along just fine with naughty-word-free us. My sister and I never so much as cringed at what we were hearing on a regular basis during that voyage.

We had a lot of fun with our new friends, just running around the ship. Often we all stood at the railings watching the scenery when we were near land and that included the skyline of Shanghai. None of us knew why the USS CHAUMONT had come there. We asked Mrs. Lambert, but she had no more idea than we did. All we knew was that our ship had steamed up the Whangpoo, and moored off the Shanghai Bund close to the battleship USS AUGUSTA, the United States flagship. We could hear the pop-pop-pop of guns going off outside the city.

I supposed I should have been terrified. But I wasn't at all. Not even the least bit nervous. We were on an American ship, weren't we? A bullet wouldn't have the nerve to hit us! It turned out that that night a shell hit the AUGUSTA, although we didn't know about it until after we had left Shanghai. We never did know why we were in a war zone in the first place, although always believed that it must have been for a very good reason.

Several of us were leaning over the railing that morning, when we spotted something in floating by in the river. We all tried to guess what it was.

"It's just an old log."

"I think it's a bundle of hay."

We all peered harder. What it was, was a body. It was the body of a man with his hands and feet tied.

"That's the way they get rid of people." "Yeah, they just tie them up, and throw them in the river."

"Alive." "Yeah."

Nobody needed to ask who the "they" was.

We all knew it was the Japanese who had invaded China. We watched the body float on down the river until it was lost amidst the boats and the sampans. Then we went back to whatever it was we were doing, and nothing more was said about it. But we all knew we had just rubbed right up close to the Japanese "incident." Only we called it a war.

As it turned out, the officer's wife and her daughters never appeared, so we never did have to give up our cabin.

We finally stood at the railings of the ship as it pulled into the dock in Manila. Mother and Father were standing there looking up and waving to us. I can only imagine how they must have felt. After all, as Mother told us, she truly believed they would never see us again.

CHAPTER XIV

The Philippines
Baguio, Boarding School And
Baloots

"If you two don't behave, you will go to boarding school!"

Boarding school! The ultimate threat! How many parents have used it, I wonder? I believe the threat was made to us probably because were having a sisterly squabble. I'm sure it was nothing worse than that, as we certainly never did anything remotely "bad" by today's standards. However, Mother felt that we probably could not tolerate going to school in the Manila heat, so we were taken at once to the cool mountain town of Baguio. There we entered The Brent School. A dreaded boarding school! After that, the boarding-school threat could never be used again. Not on me at any rate.

By then, what with our summer at Peitaho on our own, capped by an exciting escape from China by destroyer, I was well over separation- from-parents anxieties. I was ready for any adventure life could hand me, even boarding school.

We drove from the train station through groves of towering pine trees to reach the school, arriving at the girl's dormitory. It was late in the evening. The girls were all by then in their rooms, but we were welcomed by the matron into a large, warm, softly lit room, paneled in pine. Everything smelled of fresh, clean pine, outside and inside the buildings.

My sister and I were introduced to the cozy room we were to share, with two beds, two closets, and two desks. The bathroom was right down the hall, and the next morning that's where we were welcomed by other girls in the dormitory.

Classes were all in a building that we reached by walking up a rustic path to the top of a gentle hill. On the way we passed the building that was the gymnasium, and one where we had all our meals.

On the way, we also passed the school chapel. Our religious experiences had been spotty at best, mostly being taken to Sunday schools once in a while, which were held in plain, bare-bones rooms. The Brent School chapel was warm and welcoming, with the scent of pine mingled with the wax of burning candles. I had the new experience of kneeling on a bench for prayers. I even had the new experience of passing out completely one early morning when, as a member of Daughters of the King, I had to attend communion before breakfast.

A more entertaining moment came when Betty, one of my newfound friends with a rare sense of humor, arrived at church without the twenty-five centavos she usually put in the collection plate, as did the rest of us. So she pulled out what she had brought.

"Well, there goes my fifty!" she moaned, as the collection plate was carried up to the altar.

I had a miserable time trying to repress giggles for the rest of the solemn service. The reason was that the "fifty" wasn't fifty pesos, as one would have thought. Turned out it was fifty centavos, not exactly a king's ransom even in those days.

Punishment for wrongdoing at Brent School was spending Saturday morning carrying pine logs up a hill, five at a time. Goody two shoes that I had always been in school, it didn't seem that I've ever have the pleasure of that experience. But I was wrong.

"Ninety-nine beer bottles a-hanging on the wall, Ninety-nine beer bottles a-hanging on the wall. If one beer bottle should happen to fall, There's be ninety-eight beer bottles a- hanging on the wall."

Betty, a good friend of ours, Joyce, and I, were in Betty's room belting out this song at the top of our lungs one Saturday afternoon.

We had about reached eight-five beer bottles when the music teacher appeared at the door. She told us that we were to stop at once.

"Don't you girls know you are disturbing a music lesson?" she said sternly.

We all shrugged and looked sidewise at one another. Who knew?

I think we forgot to say, and should have, how sorry we were, because the following Saturday we all got blue slips sentencing us to a half hour woodpile.

"For being noisy during music lesson," read the slips.

So later that Saturday morning, Betty, Joyce and I lugged heavy, splintery pine logs, five trips, five logs at a time up and down the hill. Of course, there were others doing it as well, mostly boys. It was actually rather fun.

At Brent School was where I was introduced to boy-girl dancing. While we were there, the school held a barn dance in the gym. I was actually invited by a boy to go as his date. The problem was that he didn't know that he was supposed to dance with me. Once we slid down the slide, which was the way we all arrived at the dance, he took off and never came back. A senior boy must have seen what was happening, and asked me to dance. I supposed I should have been insulted, but I didn't know enough to realize that I ought to be. And, after all, I didn't like the boy anyway. Which might explain it.

On some Saturdays, a bus took us to the Baguio market. There I had a chance to spend my two-peso-a-week allowance at the market stalls. We were told that the people who owned them were Igorots, descendants of headhunters. I bought two carved wood figures and two woven belts. When I returned to the dormitory, I was teased and told what I'd bought were Igorot maternity belts. I wasn't worried about it. I, having turned fifteen, now knew there was no such thing as "love babies," and that, unfortunately, what Bradley had revealed to me was probably true. My maternity belts were just that, maternity belts, and my owning them didn't mean a thing.

I tried out for a play at Brent School, and won the lead role. But I never got to be in the play, because it seemed that we were going to return to Shanghai. I didn't want to leave Brent School and the good friends I'd made there, but there wasn't much chance our parents would leave us behind in the Philippines while they returned to China.

Arrangements were made for us to return to Manila with missionary friends who always traveled in the lowest train class because it was the least expensive way. After traveling in a hold at the bottom of ship, riding on hard wooden benches in a train car packed with peasant bodies was nothing to us. The only thing I minded was baloots, which a number of the Filipino passengers were enjoying all around us. Baloots, our friends informed us, were egg shells holding ducks or chickens just before they are hatched. Half-hatched chickens and ducks? No, thank you. Fortunately, our friends had brought a basket with our own lunch. And no baloots, thank you very much!

CHAPTER XV

China The Closing Curtain

We had one last adventure in the Philippines before leaving Manila. I have no idea what prompted our mother and father to do this, but they took to us to Pagsanjan. There, with my sister and I in one canoe, and the two of them in the other, we shot the famous rapids. Well, we didn't exactly do it. We were in the hands of the amazingly skilled Pagsanjan boatmen and all we had to do was sit in the canoes safely enjoying the thrills. It was an exciting end to our stay in the Philippines.

After that, we boarded a luxurious Italian liner and headed back to Shanghai. Poor us!

So back we went to the Shanghai American School where I completed my freshman year. My high school crush was still there, and so Geraldine and I picked right back up where we'd left off reporting our dreams and all the rest.

"You will have to have Amah go with you," Mother said when I was preparing to make my first visit to Geraldine's house where we were to discuss our latest romantic interludes.

"I don't need Amah," I said.

"But Amah always goes with you," said Mother.

Had she forgotten? I was fifteen years old. I had been without parents or Amah for months now. I had sailed on a U.S. Navy destroyer and been close enough to a war to hear guns popping. I had even survived boarding school!

But perhaps it was hard for her to forget that I was no longer a puny little anemic creature, afraid of Chinese funeral horns and third grade. So I allowed Amah to trail along with me. Once, at any rate.

The following summer could hardly compare to the last one. It was dull and uneventful. Mother wouldn't have let us out of her sight for "all the tea in China" at that point. So we went swimming in the French Club pool and just hung around the apartment. I had been given an accordion for Christmas, and everyone thought I should have accordion lessons along with piano lessons. I don't remember ever learning a single piece on either instrument. I may have been smart in school, but that's as far as it went.

A month after school started, we left for America. Although our mother and father were to return, my sister and I had left China forever. We had crossed the Pacific Ocean in an ocean liner for the last time.

There would be no more throwing colored paper serpentine over the railings as our ship pulled away from the docks.

No more Honolulu, our first thrilling stop on the way to America. Papaya and pineapple for breakfast aboard ship the next morning.

No more standing on the deck getting goose bumps as the ship's band played, *California, Here I Come!*

There would now be a whole new life with only a kaleidoscope of memories from China. An Amah's protecting hand reaching out to me. Coolie and I listening to No Matter How Young the Prune May Be, He's Always Full of Wrinkles. A glistening ice Buddha, and swinging up a mountain in a sedan chair. Conversations with Dossofoo in the kitchen. The mouth-watering smell of bau jaodzes wafting up the stairs at Chinese New Year's. Wonk puppies, ice cream cones and petit fours from Kiessling & Bader. Coolies singing aiya hoa by the river outside a school wall. Trains passing villages and curious small children with bright slanted eyes and slit trousers. Traveling salesmen with magic bundles. The rice-paste modeling man with magic fingers. Donkeys and scissor grinders and rickshaw rides on dusty roads.

And finally, there is the junk I saw sailing down the river in the middle of one night, a the water in total serene silence. For some reason I will never be able to explain, that, for me, will always be . . . China.

"Do you think our childhood in China was really different?" my sister asks me one day.

"I don't know," I reply. "What do you think?" My sister shrugs.

"Well, it seems to me that everyone's childhood is different," I say.

"But perhaps ours was really more different than some," replies my sister.

I think about this a moment, "Perhaps it was," I say. "Perhaps it really might have been."

And we go on our way in our saddle shoes and swinging pleated skirts to our new American high school.

A LOOK BACKWARD

When I grew up, I was to write books for children. One of them came from the time I lived in Tientsin, when I was eleven. The name of that book was CAN DO, MISSY CHARLIE, chosen by the Literary Guild as much, I think, because of my relationship to my sister as because of my "different" childhood growing up in China.

The other book was VICTORIA. This is a boarding school story in which I took Brent School, Baguio, and transported it to upper New York state. People have asked me the question I'm sure many writers are asked, "Are you in any of your books?"

They seem to think I am Charlotte in CAN DO, MISSY CHARLIE. Not at all, I am much more Dylis in VICTORIA, who is even afraid to cross a street without holding her friend Victoria's hand. And who, additionally, is madly in love with Victoria's handsome father. Anyone who has managed to read my true story, would probably have to agree.

MY OTHER BOOKS

PEPPERMINTS IN THE PARLOR
(Winner of the William Allen White Award)

THE PERILS OF PEPPERMINTS

THE TWIN IN THE TAVERN
(Mystery Writers of America EDGAR award winner)

COUSINS IN THE CASTLE
(EDGAR nominee)

SPARROWS IN THE SCULLERY
(EDGAR award winner)

GHOSTS IN THE GALLERY
(EDGAR nominee)

SECRET IN ST. SOMETHING
(ALA ten best mysteries)

THE BARREL IN THE BASEMENT

CLAUDIA

HELLO, CLAUDIA

CLAUDA AND DUFFY

ANDREW THE BIG DEAL

THE SECRET SUMMER OF L.E.B.

THE TROUBLE WITH MISS SWITCH

MISS SWITCH TO THE RESCUE

MISS SWITCH ONLINE

PALMER PATCH

JULIA AND THE THIRD BAD THING

PERFECT ACRES

HAWKINS

HAWKINS AND THE SOCCER SOLUTION

THE CONTEST KID AND THE BIG PRIZE

ARGYLE

www.ingramcontent.com/pod-product-compliance
Lightning Source LLC
Chambersburg PA
CBHW031359040426
42444CB00005B/355